Florida Spring Training

Your Guide To Touring The
Grapefruit League

Alan Byrd

Florida Spring Training

Your Guide To Touring The
Grapefruit League

Published by The Intrepid Traveler
P.O. Box 531, Branford, CT 06405

Copyright © 2007 by Alan Byrd
Additional research by Alexis Elder
Third Edition
Printed in Canada.
Book Jacket: George Foster, Foster & Foster, Inc.
Maps designed by Evora Taylor
ISBN13: 978-1-887140-68-3
ISBN10: 1-887140-68-9

International Standard Serial Number: 1552-8790

Cover Photo: Roger Dean Stadium. ©Roger Dean Stadium, used with permission.

Publisher's Cataloging in Publication Data. Prepared by librarian Dorothy L. Swerdlove.
Byrd, Alan
  Florida spring training: your guide to touring the Grapefruit League. 3rd ed. Branford, CT: Intrepid Traveler, copyright 2007.
  First ed. published 2004.
  PARTIAL CONTENTS: Foreword by Mike Stanley. –Atlanta Braves. –Baltimore Orioles. –Boston Red Sox. –Cincinnati Reds. –Cleveland Indians. –Detroit Tigers. –Florida Marlins/St. Louis Cardinals. –Houston Astros. –Los Angeles Dodgers. –Minnesota Twins. –New York Mets. –New York Yankees. –Philadelphia Phillies. –Pittsburgh Pirates. –Tampa Bay Devil Rays. –Toronto Blue Jays. –Washington Nationals.
  1. Spring training (baseball)--Florida. 2. Baseball fields--Florida--Guidebooks. 3. Florida--Description and travel--Guidebooks. 4. Baseball teams--United States/Canada. 5. Grapefruit League.
  I. Title. II. Title: Your guide to touring the grapefruit league. III. Stanley, Mike. IV. Intrepid Traveler.
  796.35709

Dedications

First and foremost, to my wife, Melissa, for having the patience to spend her spring break watching her least favorite sport.

To my son, Brandon, in whom I hope to inspire a love of Spring Training.

And to Susan Lundine, who continually encouraged me in my dreams of writing a book.

Alan Byrd

About the Author

ALAN BYRD is the director of sales, marketing, and public relations for McCree Inc., an Orlando-based architecture and construction firm. Prior to that, Byrd was the director of circulation sales and marketing for the *Orlando Business Journal*. He was also an award-winning reporter for the *OBJ* for 10 years, covering Central Florida's sports, tourism, and transportation industries. In 1998, his reporting of the Moscow Circus was named the best business story in the United States by the Society of Business Editors and Writers.

Alan contributes his marketing and organizational skills to community organizations and charities, including the Central Florida Zoo, the Valencia Foundation, several Chambers of Commerce, and the Coastal Conservation Association, where he serves as president of the Orlando chapter.

In his spare time, Alan is an avid fisherman and singer. He performs with the Barefoot Underground at the Loaded Hog in downtown Orlando, and for various charities. He has two children, Brandon and Abigail, and his wife, Melissa, patiently tolerates his baseball mania.

Florida Spring Training is his first book.

Table of Contents

Itinerary Maps

Foreword

by
Mike Stanley

Ah, Spring Training. The crack of the bat. The smell of new leather and pine tar. The umpire's first call of "Play ball!" The renewed hope that this will be the year for your favorite team.

I would be hard pressed to find two other words, which when paired together, conjure up so many different emotions for me. Excitement, nervousness, and elation — just to name a few.

These feelings started when I was a kid growing up in Fort Lauderdale, where the New York Yankees came to train for six weeks. They would be lived out during my fifteen seasons as a professional player.

My Spring Training experiences began early in life. As a young boy, I went to the games with many hopes and aspirations, as most kids did: to seek an autograph, watch my favorite players, and maybe, if I was lucky, either catch or run down a foul ball. Oh, and there was also the food. Back then it was peanuts, popcorn, Cracker Jacks, or the ever popular stadium dog. Nowhere on earth did a hot dog taste better than at the ballpark. I would go to the game with my father, my brother, or my friends. However I could get there, I would go. It was March and it was time for Spring Training games. I sat in the stands watching the games, aspiring to, one day, be out there playing the game I loved and signing my own name on baseballs and gloves.

That dream would come true in the spring of 1986. The Texas Rangers had signed me in the June draft the year before. I would be going to Spring Training in Pompano Beach, Florida, just fifteen minutes from Fort Lauderdale. I would be able to live at home and play in front of my family and friends.

It was my first Spring Training, it was Big League camp, and I was both nervous and excited about showing off my talents to the Ranger organization. Like most rookies, I didn't stay long, but I didn't care. I was there long enough to hit a home run and sign a lot of those autographs that I had longed to do as a kid.

I spent only one Spring Training season in Pompano Beach. The Rangers moved their training site to Port Charlotte on the west coast of Florida in 1987. It was here, in 1988, that I experienced the thrill of making the Major League team out of Spring Training.

In 1992, I ended my tenure with the Rangers and signed as a free agent with the New York Yankees. That's right. Come spring, I was in camp with the same team that I had come to see as a kid. I was now playing on the same field that I had dreamed of playing on as a child sitting in the stands.

Hollywood could not have improved on the script. Reggie Jackson was there. Ron Guidry was there and would throw batting practice. And my favorite, Whitey Ford, joined us. I will never forget this legend on the backfield shagging balls or feeding a curveball machine. This was a Hall of Famer! Most greats of the game simply put on a uniform for Spring Training and are there to be seen. Whitey was there to help us and make us better. I doubt you could find another player of his greatness with more humility.

I was lucky enough to spend the next three years training with the Yankees in Fort Lauderdale. Lucky because I was playing in my hometown and lucky because I was playing for the most celebrated and storied team in baseball history. We played in front of packed crowds every game thanks, in part, to what we locals call "snowbirds." South Florida attracts an enormous number of Northeasterners who either retire here or come down simply to escape the winter. It seemed like most were Yankees fans.

In spring 1996, I headed back to the west coast of Florida to Fort Myers when I signed with the Boston Red Sox. I would spend four out of my last five springs there. The only exception was in 1998, when I was in Dunedin as a member of the Toronto Blue Jays.

Each of the fifteen years of Spring Training brought different expectations and goals. My first two years I knew I had no shot at making the team. I was there simply to take it all in and experience professional baseball. From 1988 to 1992, I successfully made the team out of Spring Training based on my performance. From 1993 to 2000, I knew at the start of Spring Training that I would be on the team. Consequently, my mindset going into and during the six weeks of Spring Training changed over time.

For example, when trying to make a team, I focused extra hard on each practice and at bat during the games. Would I do something today to help my chances or would I find myself on a minor league roster the next day? For a lot of those years the answer wasn't clear until the last few days of camp. As a rookie, Spring Training statistics matter. Six weeks sometimes isn't enough time to showcase your talents.

Conversely, the years I knew I was going north with the team I viewed each practice and at bat merely as preparation for the season. As a veteran, it's all about making sure you have your timing and swing down before the season starts. Six weeks seems like an eternity. However, no matter where I was in my career, I went in trying to set goals higher than I achieved the year before for both myself and the team I played for. Where you are in life matters, too. I married my wife, Erin, in 1988, my first year in the Majors. We now have four children, Ryan, born in 1989, Tanner in 1993, Jenna in 1994, and Jake in 2001. I refer to those years to highlight where I was in my career. I also mention my family because having children made me realize that baseball was no longer the most important thing in my life.

It used to be that I couldn't wait for Spring Training to start. The off-season couldn't go by fast enough. As I got older and had a family that might or might not join me when I left for camp, the off-seasons were never long enough. When I arrived in camp, however, I did so knowing that I had a job to do and I tried to prepare myself as best I could.

I hope this gives you a better understanding of what the

Spring Training experience is all about in relation to where a player is in his career. You may now understand why the younger players may seem to hustle and care more. Don't get me wrong. The older players are trying; nobody likes to fail. They just have a different agenda for preparing themselves to play a schedule that sees them competing in 162 games in 182 days.

So get out there and enjoy yourself. Root for your favorite team. If you can, take a child or two and allow them to dream like I did. And forget the sushi and the gourmet food. There's still nothing like that good ol' stadium dog!

Introduction

As long as I can remember, I've always looked forward to the beginning of March. While many people look to the month as the end of the cold snaps that hit the Sunshine State, I always looked forward to the sights and sounds of baseball, the smell of freshly cut grass, and sitting in the sunshine, my face turning red for the first time in the new year.

March is special because it brings the boys of summer to my back yard. March signals Spring Training, the annual ritual performed by Major League Baseball. Every year, professional baseball teams make small and large cities in Florida their home for one month. One precious month that annually fills my head with hundreds of lifelong memories.

For the teams, Spring Training represents a new beginning, a time when any one of them could be starting its pilgrimage to the World Series. The players seem to be different. They don't have their game face on. They're accessible and converse with the fans. They don't seem to be there to win; they come to Florida to prepare.

For me, Spring Training represents the best Major League Baseball has to offer. For just a few dollars, I'm able to spend an afternoon with the heroes I read about and watch on television all summer long. I might even have the chance to meet the superstars of my youth.

My first Spring Training memory actually comes from my father, because I was too young to remember it. Since I lived in Boston as a young boy, the Red Sox were and still are my favorite team. I would trade any baseball card with my neighbor just to have the card of a relief pitcher from the Red Sox. And, most of all, I liked Jim Rice. Outfielder Jim Rice had it all. He was cool. He could swing the bat. He made great plays. He was the personification of the Red Sox to me.

When I was in third grade, we moved to Orlando. I was lucky. The Red Sox trained in Winter Haven's Chain of Lakes Park when I was growing up. It was just an hour or so from my Orlando home, so my father and I would make an annual pilgrimage to see the Red Sox up close.

After one game, I had my chance to meet my hero. Jim Rice stood nearby. Getting an autograph would be no problem. I could just walk up to him and ask. There's no way he would say no.

But, on the way, I was stopped. Not by some bouncer or security guard. No, Hall-of-Famer Carl Yastremski stood in my path. For those who don't know, Yastremski represents the Red Sox more than anyone outside of Ted Williams. He played with the team over three decades, setting most of the team records. During the Red Sox glory years, the mid-1970s, Yaz was the man.

On this day, however, Carl Yastremski stood between Jim Rice and me. He looked down at me and said: "Son, Jimmy had a bad game today. It might be best if you didn't get his autograph today." My response: "OK." I then walked away, not asking Carl Yastremski for his signature. After all, I wanted Jim Rice. He was my hero.

Over the years, I've created dozens of Spring Training memories that just couldn't be had any other place in the sporting world. For instance, one time while I was waiting for some friends at Chain of Lakes Park, Pete Rose pulled into his parking spot driving a big red Cadillac. I was standing two feet away from the driver side door. He popped out of the car and I got his autograph.

Another time, at Boardwalk and Baseball in Haines City, I sat on a grassy hill a foot from the field and spent 20 minutes talking with Paul Quantrill, a pitcher for the Red Sox. We talked about the previous season. We talked about the upcoming season. We talked about his pitching style and why he was in the bullpen and not a starter.

Lately, I've been able to share similar experiences with my son, Brandon. While he hasn't become the baseball fan I was at his age, he still goes to Spring Training with me and enjoys the hot dogs, the peanuts, and meeting the players.

It was at a Spring Training game that Brandon got his first autograph. I had bought him a Houston Astros pennant at Osceola County Stadium in Kissimmee. The small park has a wonderful area for getting autographs and, in the spirit of Spring Training, the players are more than happy to oblige.

My son walked up to the fence area where players and fans congregate. He waited his turn, pen and pennant in hand. One of the Astros players walked up and Brandon proceeded to ask: "Can I have my autograph?" The player smiled, handed him the pennant and pen back and said sure, with a chuckle.

Researching this book has created dozens of new memories of baseball experienced with my son and my wife, Melissa. For instance, at the first game of the 2003 season, while I was researching the first edition, I caught a foul ball from Hideki "Godzilla" Matsui, the then-rookie right fielder from Japan. I spent several games, including one standing in the rain, trying to get Godzilla to sign the ball.

Later, in Jupiter, St. Louis Cardinals great Lou Brock stood in the dugout. After I explained the importance of Lou Brock to Brandon, he decided to try and get Brock's autograph. He succeeded after several minutes of talking and pleading with Brock. Later that same day, actor John Goodman was walking out of the bathroom as I was walking in. He signed Brandon's ticket.

Lately, however, the face of Spring Training is changing. While experiences like the one with Lou Brock still await some Spring Training fans, they are becoming fewer and fewer. Each year one or two Spring Training sites change or are remodeled, and in many cases, the newer parks are too similar to their big league counterparts to foster the best of Spring Training experiences. As municipalities try to lure teams to their city, they throw in any and all perks they can. This, of course, makes sense because Spring Training is big business. Nearly 1.5 million people visit Spring Training in Florida each year, pumping over $400 million into the state's economy. The problem is, in their eagerness to woo teams, the municipalities in many cases ignore the fans' priorities.

It's not that the new stadiums present a bad experience. They offer a different experience. For instance, in the Tampa Bay area, there are four ballparks. Each gives the visitor a different experience, ranging from the intimacy of Dunedin's Knology Park to the massive number of food choices at Legends Field in Tampa. And each offers a different experience before and after the game. If you go to St. Petersburg, you're going to have plenty to do before and after, while in Clearwater, you're going to the stadium to watch a ballgame; there's little to do around the ballpark.

The same holds true in any of the pockets of Spring Training, whether it's the Gulf Coast, the East Coast, Central Florida, or Tampa-St. Petersburg. Each park presents a different feel and a different experience. One stadium might be fantastic for the die-hard baseball fan, but the most boring place alive for the first-time guest. Other stadiums appeal to both.

Each March, I visit every Spring Training site in Florida. I taste every stadium's hot dog and every specialty food. I try to get an autograph at every park and I read every program. Believe me, each place is different.

The purpose of this book is to share my findings with you so that you'll be able to plan your trip to Spring Training with an understanding of what each ballpark offers you.

How This Book Is Organized

Chapter One offers a short history of Spring Training in Florida, with an emphasis on its traditions. Chapters Two through Eighteen cover each of Florida's Spring Training stadiums in detail, with rundowns on the overall feel of the ballpark and specifics on the parking, tickets, program, seating, shade, food, drink, and souvenir merchandise. In these chapters, you will also find directions to the ballpark and helpful information on nearby restaurants, sports bars, attractions, and lodging.

Chapter Nineteen ranks the stadiums on each of five key factors (intimacy, autographing opportunities, comfort, food, and style). Chapter Twenty lays out five different week-long itineraries, complete with things to do outside the ballparks, for those of you who want to build an entire vacation around Florida Spring Training. Finally, the Indexes will help you look up the stadiums that interest you and see at a glance which stadiums you visit on each of the five itineraries.

Stadium Specifics

Your experience in a ballpark depends on a number of factors, ranging from the weather and the sheer excitement of the game to the food, seats, ticket price, and so on. I can't do anything about the first two, but my rundowns on the following will help you determine what to expect at any given park so that you choose the experience that suits you best. For example, you may be a Yankees fan, but the experience you're looking for from a Spring Training game may better be found in the Phillies' Clearwater spring home rather than the Yankees' home field in Tampa. Whatever your taste in baseball, I'll help you satisfy it.

Each observation in the book is based on what I saw that day, and what was offered during that season. Please note that while stadiums themselves rarely change, the food, souvenir offerings, and entertainment change on a regular basis.

Fast Facts. Addresses, phone numbers, and web sites.

Getting There. Driving directions from the closest highway.

Parking. How close is the parking lot? Check here to see how long it will take you to get from your car to the stadium entrance and how much it costs to park. Here I also note any special tips you should know before you set out for the stadium, such as special lots for special sections of the ballpark and transportation and parking alternatives.

Tickets. Are tickets available — and affordable? Some teams sell out (see "Rules of the Game," below); others usually still have tickets at gametime. Check this section to see if you need to buy tickets in advance, far in advance, or can pick them up at gametime. Also check here for ticket prices.

Price Note: 2007 prices for tickets have not been announced by most parks as this book goes to press. Figure that they will likely be slightly higher than the prices listed here.

Programs. Programs! Get your souvenir programs! Is the program worth the price? Check here to see what it costs and what it contains. I favor programs that include photos and numerical listings of the players (so that it's easy to identify who's who on the field), articles on Spring Training, and scorecards.

Seats. Can you find your seat easily? Each stadium chapter includes a seating diagram. Check your tickets against the diagram and my sage advice before heading into the stadium. Seats are a lot easier to find in some stadiums than in others. And once you're seated it can be quite a trek to get to the concessions or to the best spots for getting autographs.

Shade. Is there any shade? The Florida sun is fierce, even in March. The amount of shade in any given stadium depends on its orientation and roofing. In March, the afternoon sun is in the southern sky, so stadiums that face south and have little roofing have little or no shade. Check this section to find out how much sunblock you'll need.

Food & Drink. It's time to satisfy those hunger pangs and quench your thirst! What's available? Do the hot dogs snap? Is the beer really cold? A ballpark's food and drink are almost as important to baseball fans as bats and balls. Look here to see what's offered, and whether the stadium has a specialty that shouldn't be missed.

Note: For security — and better profits — none of the stadiums allows fans to bring in food or beverages.

Souvenirs. You can't leave Spring Training without a souvenir. What's unusual here? You can get bats, balls, baseball caps, and t-shirts at any Grapefruit League stadium. Look here to find the stadium's unique offerings (if any). Infant hats, anyone? Bobble head dolls?

Autographs. How easy is it to get an autograph? Where are the best spots to get them? Check here.

A Game or an Experience? Is there anything doing at the ballpark other than the game? Sure you're there for baseball. But many stadiums offer entertainment and activities to keep the family entertained. Check here to find out what's on.

Up Close & Personal? Can you reach out and touch the players? Check here to see how close you will feel to the players from your seats or the autographing areas.

Getting Away. How long will it take you to get out of the parking lot and back on the road after the game? Find out here.

Before & After the Game. Look here for suggestions on places to eat, sports bars, and things to see and do near the stadium.

Hotels Near the Ballpark. Nuff said.

Chapter 1

A Spring Training Primer

Spring Training has been a part of the Florida landscape nearly as long as orange groves, pink flamingos, and bright sunny beaches. Well, maybe not that long, but close.

The first official Spring Training event took place over a century ago when the Washington Capitals decided to prepare for the 1888 baseball season in Jacksonville, Florida. To put that in perspective, the New York Yankees didn't yet exist and Babe Ruth wouldn't be born for another seven years.

Spring Training in Florida didn't last long then; the Capitals failed to return the following year. Spring Training wouldn't come back until 1903, when Hall of Fame manager Connie Mack brought his Philadelphia Athletics to Jacksonville to train. But this time it took hold. Slowly other teams followed the Athletics to Florida. Over the course of time, a league came together and dubbed itself the Grapefruit League.

The modern era of Spring Training traces its roots to 1948 in Vero Beach. At that time, Dodgers' executives Branch Rickey, Walter O'Malley, and Bud Holman decided that Florida could be more than just a place their Major League team visited to prepare for the season. It could be a year-round baseball school, a place every player in the Dodgers organization could visit, practice, and leave a better player for the experience.

To carry out their vision, the Dodgers' executives bought a large plot of land in tiny Vero Beach and built a sprawling campus that could house the entire organization. It included dormitories, health facilities, and nearly every type of training complex available. They named it Dodgertown.

That campus still stands in Vero Beach, although the city recently constructed updated facilities to help the team train. A trip to Florida for Spring Training is incomplete without a visit to Dodgertown. It is the shrine of Spring Training.

Not surprisingly, once they saw Dodgertown, other teams wanted similar facilities. Although nothing like the Dodger campus was built for several years, Spring Training took hold over the next few decades and the teams' host cities reaped growing financial benefits from the annual influx of visitors from the north.

Indeed, most cities in Florida have hosted a Major League Baseball team at one time or another. In the early years, training activities centered mostly around Jacksonville. They spread to locations around the state as more teams trekked south for training in the early spring and more Florida cities took a liking to baseball in March and the dollars it brought them. Fort Myers, now home to the Minnesota Twins and the Boston Red Sox, has held Grapefruit League Spring Training contests since 1925. Even cities as far flung as Pensacola have held Grapefruit League events.

Over the decades, millions of fans have flocked to Florida in March just to watch a few baseball games. For many people it's become an annual ritual, passed on from generation to generation. Why? Because traditionally there has been something special about Spring Training that is not found in any other sports arena or in Major League Baseball itself after the boys of summer head north. Part of it is the intimacy. While most people will never get the opportunity to sit behind home plate at a Major League Baseball stadium, anybody can sit close enough at Spring Training to spit sunflower seeds onto the field. It's also an inexpensive treat. While tickets next to the field in a Major League Baseball stadium can cost up to $100 or more — if you can get them — you're going to be hard pressed to spend more than $20 on a ticket to a Grapefruit League game in most stadiums. In fact, you'll find places where you can get good seats for less than $10.

But, perhaps more than anything else, the real attraction

of Spring Training is the attitude of the players. While many people view professional athletes as distant and aloof, in Spring Training, most are anything but. They are willing to talk to fans. They sign plenty of autographs. They joke with each other. They look like they are having fun. At least they used to.

Unfortunately, Spring Training is changing in many places. The change began in the late 1980s when the team owners realized there was money to be made and better facilities to be had, thanks to the ardor of fans and the visitor dollars they bring to the teams' Spring Training communities. As a result, the days of a team like the Dodgers buying land and building a large campus for itself were over. Team managers started pressuring cities and counties to build them updated stadiums and training facilities at taxpayer expense or lose the team to another locality. It was now up to local governments to make sure the teams continued to visit every March.

The result has been an intense competition for teams that has generated constant change. Only five of the eighteen teams that practice in Florida are training at the same place they practiced in 1980. Cities such as Winter Haven lost teams they had hosted for decades and had to woo others. Others, such as Orlando, Daytona Beach, Plant City, and Port Charlotte, have been left without Spring Training events. Three teams have left the state and now practice in Arizona in the Cactus League.

The competition for teams has brought about another unfortunate development for fans like you and me: a vastly different experience of Spring Training in many places. Nowadays, you have to search to find stadiums that let you enjoy the relaxed intimacy that was once a staple of the Spring Training experience. For one thing, it is extremely difficult to get close to the players in a number of the newer parks. As more and more people travel to see Spring Training, bigger and bigger parks are being built. Fans who buy the cheaper seats in these parks will find themselves a lot farther away from the players than they used to be, while fans who like the prime seats — the kind they can't get or can't afford in their Major League park back home — will find them harder to come by. The reason: the bigger stadiums tend to push corporate season ticket purchases, leaving fewer prime seats for the average fan.

As a result, you can find yourself looking at a "sold out" section and see plenty of empty box seats.

Another reason for the lack of intimacy at many of the newer stadiums is that it is hard to come into contact with players. While you will be able to see the players joke with one another, you won't be able to get close enough to hear the punch line. The architects apparently think that it is good to keep the fans away from the players. For instance, in most of the newer stadiums, players enter and exit the field through the dugout, just as they do in the Major League Baseball stadiums. Traditionally, players have entered and left Spring Training fields through a door in the outfield wall, putting them in close contact with fans.

That's not to say that all the new stadiums are bad or give a horrible Spring Training experience. Quite the opposite is true. All of the stadiums, new and old, have something good and something bad about them. The question is, do you want to have an experience similar to "traditional" Spring Training or a Spring Training experience that is similar to the one you will find in any Major League Baseball park?

In a traditional ballpark, you are usually going to find older chairs and facilities. You'll also be closer to the players and have more opportunities for autographs. You'll sacrifice on food options, but you'll make up for it when the catcher tosses your son a baseball.

In the newer parks, you're going to have plastic seats, usually with cup holders. You'll have a choice of sushi or smoothies. You'll miss getting Derek Jeter's autograph, but you won't miss a stat with the Jumbotron relaying data and images of your favorite players throughout the game.

Four stadiums successfully blend the two experiences. They are Fort Myers' City of Palms Park, home of the Boston Red Sox, Kissimmee's Osceola County Stadium, home of the Houston Astros, Jupiter's Roger Dean Stadium, home of both the St. Louis Cardinals and the Florida Marlins, and Clearwater's new Bright House Networks Field, home of the Philadelphia Phillies.

This book will help you determine the type of Spring Training experience you want to have and where you need to go to get it. Use it to pick the experience — or experiences — you're after and to take best advantage of the opportunities for autographs and player contact offered by the stadiums you visit.

Those of you who have been to only a few Major League Baseball games should be forewarned: Spring Training may turn you into a lifelong fan of the game. If you're unwilling to take that risk, better stick with the theme parks and swimming holes. If you're game, read on.

Rules of the Game

Wherever you head, keep the following in mind:

Season Schedule. The teams usually announce their Spring Training schedule in mid December. You will want to check it as soon as possible so you can better plan your visit to catch the teams you want to see where you want to see them. The best way to do this is to visit the individual team web sites, which I have listed in the Stadium chapters that follow.

Tickets. Tickets to most Spring Training games are available right up to game time. The exceptions are games involving the four "marquee" teams, the Boston Red Sox, New York Yankees, New York Mets, and Atlanta Braves. These teams consistently draw the biggest crowds. If you want to be assured of a seat, buy your tickets in January when single tickets go on sale.

In 2006, several Spring Training sites introduced tiered pricing systems for their tickets. Games against popular teams or games on weekends are often a couple of dollars higher than other games. This is a trend that fans will likely see throughout the Grapefruit League in coming years.

Ticket Sales. Season tickets generally go on sale by mail the day after Thanksgiving. Single ticket sales begin in January, the first Saturday after New Year's Day at many parks. You can order single tickets by mail, by fax or by Internet, or get them at the stadium ticket windows. You can also get them through such services as Ticketmaster and Ticketron. Check the team's web site for more information.

Rainouts: While Florida is relatively dry during March, there is a chance for a spring shower or two during your visit. If one hits on a game day, the stadium will make every effort to play the game; after all, a rainout means lost revenue.

But they happen. During a recent season, for instance, three games were cancelled and others were called before they became official games. In such cases, most stadiums will allow you to exchange your ticket for a game at a later date. Of course, if you are on a tight schedule, chances are you'll be out of luck because unlike in the major leagues, Spring Training games are not made up. You may be eligible for a refund, but you'll have to go to the stadium ticket office to get it.

Autographs. Most parks will allow you to get autographs from players, if the players are willing. Players are more willing to sign if you have only one or two items. Bring a pen that works on the item you want signed. For example, rollerballs work well on baseballs. Sharpies work on just about everything. Never use a pen with water-based ink.

Tip: For the best chance at an autograph, get to the park at least two hours before game time unless otherwise specified in the appropriate Stadium chapter.

Game Times. Most Spring Training games are day games. Day games usually start around 1:00 p.m., night games around 6:00 or 7:00 p.m. In most cases, the stadiums open their doors two hours before game time.

What to Bring and What to Leave Home. Wear sunscreen to any and all day games regardless of the amount of shade and consider bringing a baseball cap or hat. In Florida's sun, it can take just 15 minutes without protection to burn. Do not try to bring coolers, food, or video cameras into the game with you. They aren't allowed.

Seating Hot Spots. There are three great places to watch the game in every ballpark — behind home plate, behind the right field dugout, or behind the left field dugout. Of course, some places you'll be sitting in the sun and others you won't, but you'll never go wrong. You will always be close to the action in one of these sections.

Seeing Stars. Spring Training is not like most professional sports. If you want to see the stars play, get there when the game starts. During the first two weeks of training, many players will play three innings or fewer. As spring goes on, players stay on the field longer, but the high-profile stars rarely play a full game during the spring.

Glossary

Throughout this book, I will use terms and ideas that are common to baseball fans. For those of you who are less familiar with the structure of baseball and its stadiums, here is a glossary of terms.

Berm. A grassy hill, usually in the outfield, where people can sit or lie down to watch a baseball game.

Bleachers. A set of metallic seats, usually without armrests or backs. The bleacher sections are traditionally farther away from home plate than the rest of the seats in the stadium.

Box Seats. The best seats in the stadium, traditionally right behind home plate.

Cactus League. The Major League Baseball teams that do their Spring Training in Arizona.

Grandstand. A set of permanent seats with armrests and chair backs. These are usually the seats closest to the center of the stadium.

Grapefruit League. The Major League Baseball teams that do their Spring Training in Florida.

Home Team. The host stadium's team.

Keeping Score. Traditionally, baseball fans kept track of all the action in a type of shorthand. Today you see fewer and fewer people keeping score that way because every stadium has a scoreboard for easy reference. However, most programs include a page or two for traditional scorekeeping. Read the directions in the program if you don't know how but would like to give it a try.

Main Concourse. This is where you will find most of the stadium's concessions, souvenirs, and information. You're usually in or adjacent to the main concourse when you enter the stadium.

Main Seating Aisle. Most stadiums are designed with seats above and below this aisle. It's where you're going to head to find the section with your seat.

Non-Roster Invitee. Teams are allowed to start Spring Training with 40 people on their rosters. These are usually people who are guaranteed a contract or a spot on the Major League Baseball team. However, the teams aren't limited to playing with their roster personnel. They may invite as many players as they want to Spring Training. These "non-roster" players are often rookies or minor league players hoping to latch on with a team by proving their worth in training. Most, as Mike Stanley relates in his Foreword (above), don't last long.

On-Deck Circle. The player who is due to bat next is said to be in the on-deck circle.

Roster. A baseball team's forty players. A listing of the team's players.

Split Squad. A team composed of regular players and other, usually non-roster invitees. During the short Spring Training season, clubs will use split squads so they can play two games on the same day. This allows the club a chance to look over more aspiring players, but it works against the fans since there will be fewer stars on a split squad. To address this problem, Major League Baseball has decreed that all Spring Training games must feature a minimum of four regular players and a starting pitcher in their opening lineup.

Sticker Contests. At most stadiums, you have a chance to win something if you buy the program. The teams place some sort of sticker on a particular page in a number of programs. If you find one of the stickers, you win.

Visitors. The visiting team, or players on that team.

Chapter 2

Atlanta Braves
The Ballpark at Disney's
Wide World of Sports®
Complex
in Walt Disney World® Resort

In Spring Training circles, there are few stadiums with as much hype as Disney's. Perhaps it's the Disney magic. Here's the recipe for Spring Training a la Mickey:

- Take the basics of Spring Training.
- Take everything a Major League Ballpark has and miniaturize it.
- Add in Pixie Dust, the stuff you only find at the Magic Kingdom.
- Throw in $100 million and stir.

That's the feeling you get at this beautiful ballpark in Walt Disney World® Resort (WDW). It's not really Spring Training as its fans think of it. It's corporate America bringing its influence to bear on one of the last bastions of what's great about baseball. Yet it's done so well that if you aren't looking for a traditional Spring Training experience, you're likely to be happy here.

The ballpark isn't a terrible stadium. It's one of the most comfortable and picturesque ballparks in all of Florida, and it is the only double-decker stadium in the Grapefruit League. Watching from the second deck is an experience you'll find only at WDW, but it's not necessarily the heart of Spring Training.

The outside of the stadium is themed to look like a Spanish town, complete with a lengthy promenade. Along the promenade are sponsored exhibits, souvenir stands, and security check

© Disney

points (don't worry, you'll only have to pass through one of them on your way to your seat). Inside, you'll find roomy seats, great hot dogs, lots more concessions, and a tremendous amount of fun.

This is a large park by Grapefruit League standards, with 7,500 seats, the majority located between first and third base. It's great, however, to watch the game from the bleacher seats on the right field line, as far out as possible. Sitting here gives you a good chance to catch a foul ball (one hit a woman sitting two seats down from me). It is also one of the only places to get an autograph. On the left field side, the park has a large berm where you can enjoy the Florida sun while the kids run around. The top of both the right and left field grandstands include corporate picnic areas. During some games, you will find basketball hoops and other game paraphernalia in the picnic areas. Feel free to use them.

What sets this ballpark apart from other Spring Training venues, besides its double deck, is the entertainment it offers. Fireworks, disc jockeys, and rock music keep fans entertained and excited through all nine innings, even when the stars of the game have hit the shower. For instance, the roving microphone person will come up to someone in the stands and ask them a trivia question over the public address system. He may play "name that tune" or lead a golf game in the left field berm.

Activities like these take place in a number of stadiums, but the difference here is that Disney knows how to pick entertainers. The roving microphone man is a professional, not just a staff member who's not afraid to speak on the public address system, as is the case in most other parks.

While fans will be entertained here, they will rarely get close to the stars. This is, after all, a Major League Ballpark in miniature. And just as in Major League Baseball, players here enter the field through the dugout. They don't walk along the bleacher walls as they do in traditional Spring Training parks. In addition, the stands are higher here than they are in most Spring Training stadiums. The right field stands sit at least 20 feet above the playing surface and there is a cement wall on the grandstand fences. What it all adds up to is that fans will get autographs here only if the players are in a good mood and the fan is in the right spot — just past the dugout on the first base side.

The day I visited, pitcher John Smoltz must have spent 30 minutes signing and I managed to get his autograph. All-star outfielder Chipper Jones also signed. But that was a rarity according to many of the regulars. Only a couple of other players even came to the stands, and they stayed just five minutes or so.

While there are regulars here, this stadium is not necessarily a place you're going to find the die-hard baseball fan. Instead, expect a lot of curious tourists; this is the Walt Disney World® Resort, after all. While Spring Training attracts literally millions of tourists to Grapefruit League stadiums, the feel of the crowd here is different from that at other stadiums. You'll see lots of families and few regulars. Sure, you'll meet fans of the Atlanta Braves, complete with their thick Georgia accents, but you'll encounter far more accents from Britain, the Midwest, the Northeast, and a hodgepodge of other areas. It's really a place to talk about the newest changes to "The Twilight Zone Tower of Terror"™ in Disney-MGM Studios and how your daughter enjoyed her first ride on "it's a small world" at the Magic Kingdom.

All told, this stadium is perfect for those looking to experience a baseball game with all the creature comforts. You get a truly Major League ballpark feeling here, more than at just about any other Spring Training stadium in Florida. If you're looking to reach out and touch your favorite player, however, you'll be happier elsewhere.

Fast Facts

The Ballpark at Disney's Wide World of Sports® Complex
Lake Buena Vista, FL 32830
407-939-GAME
http://atlanta.braves.mlb.com
http://www.disneysports.com/atlantabraves

Getting There

Take I-4 to Exit 65, Osceola Parkway West, turn left at the first stop light onto Victory Way and follow it into the stadium.

Parking

Prepare to walk when you park at Disney's Wide World of Sports® Complex. The parking is at least a half a mile from the stadium — allow ten to fifteen minutes to reach the entrance. The only exception is the handicapped parking, which is fairly close. If you aren't handicapped and want to park as close to the stadium as you can, plan to arrive two hours before game time.

That's the bad news. The good news is that parking here is free. This is the only stadium in the Grapefruit League with free parking. (It's about the only thing you will find at WDW that's free.) And while it's going to take you a while to get into the stadium, Disney will see that you're entertained on the way. For instance, a baseball-uniformed sax quartet was playing along the promenade the day I visited.

Cost: Free

Tickets

You'll need to get your tickets early, preferably when they go on sale in January (see Chapter 1). While I was able to get tickets to see the Braves play the Devil Rays on short notice, there were no tickets for seats close to home plate. Also, most tickets to the big draws like the Yankees or Red Sox will be long gone by the time March rolls around.

As for the prices, this is where Disney gets its money back. Tickets here are among the more expensive in Spring Training.

Capacity: 9,500 (7,500 in the grandstand and bleachers; 2,000 on the berm)

Average Attendance: 9,498

Ticket Prices:

Lower level $22.50

Upper level & bleachers $19.50

Lawn (berm) seating $14

For Tickets: Call 407-939-GAME for group tickets, suites, and packages. Get individual game tickets through Ticketmaster or in person at Disney's Wide World of Sports® box office.

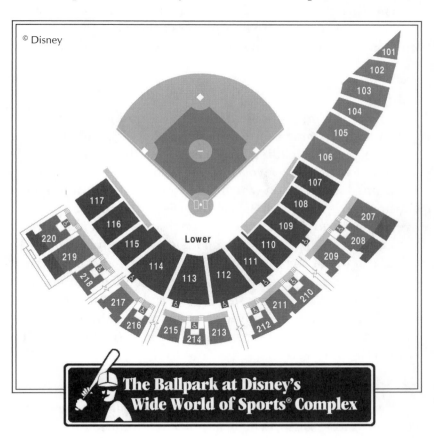

Programs

The program here is not as thick as some other Spring Training programs, but it is a worthwhile investment. It has plenty of stories, both on the baseball side of the team and the personal side. For instance, the program I got had an interesting story on several of the players' vacations. (Funny how most of those vacations took place at a Walt Disney property.) The program included a scorecard for those like myself who still like to hand score a baseball game. It included the essential numerical roster of players based on position. It also had individual mug shots of the entire team in alphabetical order. This is a feature that should be in every Spring Training program so you can start to learn who's who when you first walk into the stadium.

The Disney program also gets my award for the cheesiest feature: a centerfold with star players dressed in Disney clothing. I gotta admit, it's something no other program attempts.

Cost: $5

Seats

This is the only double-decker stadium in Spring Training, so finding your seat can be a little tricky. But the seats and the tunnels leading to them are both well marked. If you are on the lower level, turn right or left as you enter the stadium, depending on which side your seat is on, and follow the appropriate tunnel. (Of course, Disney & Company would prefer you to go through the souvenir store that's just beyond the entrance.) Or if you want, go inside the stadium and walk along the top of the lower level seats until you come to your section. For top-level seating, walking inside the stadium isn't an option because there's no inside walkway on the second level. Instead, take one of the two sets of stairs you'll find immediately past the entrance. Climb them and head down the tunnel to your seat.

Shade

If you want shade, sit at the top of the lower level. The stadium faces south, which is not advantageous for shade. The sun is in the southern sky in spring, and it shines on the field for most of the game. Your best bet would be to go for a seat on the first base side. Be aware that the top level offers no shade whatsoever until almost the end of the game when the sun goes behind the sky boxes on the right field side.

Food & Drink

The hot dogs are remarkably good at WDW — some of the best in Spring Training. But they are the same dogs you had in the WDW theme parks; so you may want to try another offering like the Grand Slam Cheeseburger. Better yet, try the truly unique offering here, the gyro. This is a fantastic sandwich. The lamb is cooked right in the booth (called "Gyro Express," it's located on the right field side) and is taken off the cooker as you place your order. Lots of meat and lots of cucumber sauce make this a do not miss item. Just be sure to grab lots of napkins.

While beer at WDW may not be exactly what Uncle Walt wanted, it is available here at the ballpark. Drink it quick before it gets warm and make sure it doesn't spill; there are no cup holders in the seat arms. If you're looking for the hard stuff, you'll find that too. The stadium has a couple of full liquor stands. The drinks they serve are strictly take-away as the stands have neither bars nor bar stools.

Note: One of the best things about the park is the several concession stands that face the field. Buying your hot dogs and beer at these stands allows you to turn and watch the game as you wait in line. Surprisingly, the lines at these stands seem to be significantly shorter than those at the stands on the outer concourse even though both offer the same food.

Souvenirs

It's easy to find a souvenir here. In fact, you may be tempted to hit the mobile souvenir stand along the walkway from the parking lot or shop the souvenir store near the ticket window even before you enter the stadium. But the only reason to stop at either is to break up your walk to the stadium. The mobile stand has a limited selection, and the store near the ticket windows ("D Sports") is generally crowded. So save your souvenir hunting for the store right inside the entrance, called Disney's Clubhouse. It's easy to find most items, and surprisingly, it's not too crowded.

The stadium store offers almost anything a baseball fan would want. Shirts, hats, baseballs, and bats abound. The prices are a little high. A baseball that costs $5 at almost every other stadium in Florida costs $8 at WDW. As you might expect, there is a Disney twist to some of the souvenirs. For instance, this is the only Spring Training stadium in which you will find Mickey Mouse-shaped pretzels.

Autographs

Getting autographs is not an easy task here. The stadium is designed to prevent access to the players. In fact, the only autographs you'll be able to get are those of players who actually come over to the stands — and that's not often with the Atlanta Braves. The only place the players visit (and only some of them, sometimes) is just past the dugout on the first base side. If you want the chance to get an autograph, hang out there. But be aware that in a further attempt to discourage autographs, the stadium chases everyone out of the sections nearest the dugouts about 30 minutes before the game, which in other stadiums is one of the best times to get an autograph.

A Game or an Experience?

In 2003, Disney installed a brighter scoreboard with a great addition, a miles-per-hour square. After every pitch, the stadium shows how fast the pitcher threw the ball. Be quick to look, as the speed doesn't stay up there long. Still, it's something that should be at every park.

Baseball Disney-style is packed with entertainment. If you like music, you'll enjoy the saxophone group. And the disc jockey type games keep people in their seats between innings. If you're looking for something to keep the tots entertained, however, get a seat on the outfield berm and let them roll down the hill. There's relatively little else for youngsters to do inside unless the basketball hoop and other game paraphernalia happen to be set up (see above) the day you visit.

Note: Outside the stadium, behind the Milk House, the multi-sports experience interactive area is open to all guests on game days.

Up Close & Personal?

You'll be hard put to get close to the players here.

Getting Away

How bad the traffic is leaving the park is always contingent on when you leave the game, and that is particularly true here. The problem comes when you try to leave the lot to head for the road. Usually, there are only one or two exits from each of the parking lots. Those exits generally lead to one road and one way out of the parking complex (although I have seen two exits open on occasion). The result, especially for big games, is thousands of cars all waiting to go through one of two exits. I've sat for more than an hour in the parking lot waiting to get out. Once you get out of the lot, it's clear sailing, as WDW has an excellent road system.

There's just one way to get around it if you drive: leave early.

Before & After the Game: Restaurants

As you'd expect at a resort that attracts millions of visitors a year, there are plenty of eateries in and around WDW. Here are a few of I recommend, grouped by location:

At Disney's Wide World of Sports® Complex

Located at the Complex entrance and less than 100 feet from the stadium, All-Star Café is one of the few remaining outlets of a now-defunct chain. Normal hours of operation during Spring Training are 11:30 a.m. to 9:00 p.m. (later after night games). The menu features the All American Classic burger and the All Star Café's famous signature ribs. Inside, there are 20-plus big screen TVs to keep you entertained while you eat.

At Disney's BoardWalk

Located on WDW property near the back entrance to Epcot theme park, the BoardWalk charges no admission and offers four full-service restaurants: the sports-themed ESPN Club, Big River Grille & Brewing Works (serving American food), Mediterranean-themed Spoodles, and the high-end seafood restaurant, Flying Fish Cafe. The first two are open for lunch and dinner; the last two only for dinner.

At Disney's Animal Kingdom Lodge

On Osceola Parkway, this Disney resort hotel is home to two restaurants with African-inspired menus, moderately priced Boma and high-end Jiko. Both are open for dinner.

At Downtown Disney

Walt Disney World® Resort's dining and entertainment complex sports a number of eateries, among them House of Blues, Bongo's Cuban Café (both moderately priced), and Wolfgang Puck's (expensive). All are open for lunch and dinner.

Note: Priority seating reservations are advisable. Call 407-939-DINE (3463). "Priority seating" doesn't guarantee you a seat at a specific time. It means you will be seated as close to your "reservation" time as possible and ahead of any walk-in patrons.

Before & After the Game: Attractions

You'll never lack for things to do at WDW. A few suggestions follow. If nothing here rings your chimes, the greater Orlando area offers literally hundreds of other things to see and do. For details on over 200 of them, check out *The Other Orlando: What to Do When You've Done Disney and Universal*, by Kelly Monaghan (www.TheOtherOrlando.com).

WDW Theme Parks

You have four to choose from, the Magic Kingdom, Disney's Animal Kingdom, Epcot, and Disney-MGM Studios. Prices listed here are from 2006, and may change without notice. Hours vary seasonally. For the latest information, visit www.disneyworld.com, or call 407-WDISNEY. One-day entry to a single park (with tax and rounded to the nearest dollar) is $67 for adults and $55 for kids 3 to 9 years old as we go to press. Disney also offers many ticket options, up to a 10-day ticket with unlimited access to all the theme parks, water parks, and DisneyQuest, a no-expiration-date feature, and other bells and whistles.

WDW Water Parks

WDW has two water parks, Typhoon Lagoon and Blizzard Beach. Hours vary seasonally. Cost with tax: Adult $37, Children (3 to 9) $31.

DisneyQuest

A four-story indoor interactive playground in Downtown Disney, it charges $37 for adults and $31 for kids 3 to 9.

Before & After the Game: Activities

WDW Golf

You have six to choose from at Walt Disney World Resort. Call 407-939-GOLF for tee times and hours and be sure to reserve your tee time well in advance. Prices are for resort guests and can vary by time of day. Non-guests can expect to pay about $10 more.

- Osprey Ridge, $155
- Eagle Pines, $155
- Magnolia, $155
- Palm, $139
- Lake Buena Vista, $109
- Oak Trail 9-hole walking course, $38 for adults, $20 for juniors (age 17 and under)

Miniature Golf Courses

- Fantasia Gardens
- Winter Summerland

Both charge about $11 plus tax for adults and $9 for children age 3 to 9.

Miscellaneous Activities

Here are a few more possibilities.

Guided fishing trips. $200 to $230 for two hours (depending on the time of day), $80 per additional hour.

Horseback riding. $32 for a 45-minute guided ride.

Tennis. Located at several WDW hotels. Courts are free for hotel guests.

Call 407-939-PLAY for reservations or information about any or all of the above.

Hotels Near the Ballpark

- Disney's Pop Century Resort (Value priced), 1050 Century Drive (right next to the sports complex)

- Disney's All Star Movies, Music and Sports Resorts (Value priced), 1991 West Buena Vista Drive
- Disney's Caribbean Beach Resort (Moderate), 900 Cayman Way
- Disney's Coronado Springs Resort (Moderate), 1000 West Buena Vista Drive
- Disney's Yacht & Beach Club Resorts (Deluxe), 1700 EPCOT Resorts Boulevard

For Walt Disney World Resort hotel reservations, call 407-W-DISNEY (934-7639). Like the rest of WDW, the resorts are located in Lake Buena Vista, Florida.

Chapter 3

Baltimore Orioles
Fort Lauderdale Stadium

Fort Lauderdale

The thing people seem to remember most about Fort Lauderdale Stadium is the leg room in the box seats. In this day and age of stadiums designed to cram in as many seats as possible, Fort Lauderdale is an anomaly. There's enough room between the box seats for even the burliest beer vendor to pass seated fans without the fans having to move.

The stadium's site is another story. Fort Lauderdale Stadium is one of the oldest in the Grapefruit League, and it appears there wasn't a lot of planning on where to place it. Or perhaps the surrounding area has simply changed a good deal in the forty plus years since it went up. Whatever the explanation, you drive through an industrial park to get to the stadium. There's nothing around it but warehouses and a corporate airport. Throughout a game at this antique stadium, the crack of the bat is drowned out by the sound of Gulfstream jets taking off and landing at the airport behind the ballpark.

First-time visitors are likely to find Fort Lauderdale Stadium confusing. It has three entrance gates, each leading to a particular part of the stadium (grandstands, left bleachers, and right bleachers). Once inside, you can't walk from one area to another; so be sure to check your seating location before you leave for the park and park accordingly. If you park by the wrong gate, you'll have a long walk to your seats.

Inside, Fort Lauderdale Stadium is a fairly traditional Spring Training park, if not one of the best designed. In the

Photo courtesy of the Baltimore Orioles.

main seating bowl (the box and reserved grandstand seats), there is only one area with restrooms, concessions, and souvenirs. (The right and left field bleachers have their own concession areas, two for the right field and one for the left.) If you want anything to eat or drink, buy it when you first get in; unlike in most Spring Training sites, there is nothing available near the seats. Once you've picked up these essentials, you'll walk up a ramp into the bowl and then to your seats. Large tropical plants (varieties you'll find only in this region of the state) line the walkway. They give you the feeling that you're going through a jungle as you make your way to your seat.

While there is little to distinguish Fort Lauderdale Stadium from many other Spring Training parks, it is one of the few parks in the Grapefruit League with bleachers outside the outfield wall. Located in right field, they're a great place to sit if you want to catch a home-run ball. Only the die-hard baseball fans sit there.

Fort Lauderdale Stadium is, in many ways, Spring Training the way it should be. While it doesn't offer the frills you'll find in many of the newer parks, it is a great place to watch a game. The players are easily accessible to the fans. Stand along the wall near home plate and you'll overhear their conversations as they take batting practice. In addition, you're very close to the diamond, especially in the box seats. In fact the players are even more accessible here because they have to walk near the grandstands to get around the batting cage for their pre-game practice. In the outfield, pitchers warm up near the bleachers, presenting yet another opportunity to get close to the players. Unlike in traditional Spring Training stadiums, however, the players here enter and exit the playing field through the dugout. This limits your access to them if you sit in the main seating bowl.

Like most South Florida stadiums, this one is filled with retirees. Some are from the Washington/Baltimore area, but most seem to be from other Northeastern locales. You'll find a significant number of regulars here who know all the players and their life stories, but not as many as you'll run into in most other Spring Training parks.

All told, don't go to Fort Lauderdale Stadium for a show. Go there to watch baseball up close and in comfort.

Fast Facts

Fort Lauderdale Stadium
1301 Northwest 55th Street
Fort Lauderdale, FL 33309
954-776-1921
http://baltimore.orioles.mlb.com

Getting There

Take I-95 to Exit 32, Commercial Boulevard West. Proceed west on Commercial to Northwest 12th Avenue (also known as Oriole Boulevard). Turn right onto Northwest 12th. It's the second stadium on the left.

Parking

There are few stadiums with parking as close to the entrance as Fort Lauderdale, provided you choose the right lot. The key is figuring out which section your tickets are in before you get to the game because each section has its own adjacent parking lot. If you park in the section near the right field bleachers and you're sitting in the left field bleachers, you'll have a long walk to your entrance gate. So double-check before you leave for the park.

The parking lots next to the stadium are fairly small. So plan to arrive early if being just a minute or two's walk to the park is important to you. If you arrive at gametime, you'll be parking across the street. Still, you won't tire walking to the game. It will take you only five to ten minutes from across the street.

If you want to see what the players drive, their parking lot is between the right field bleachers lot and the main grandstand lot.

Cost: $5

Tickets

Good seats are often available at the last minute at Fort Lauderdale Stadium. I bought my tickets two days before the game and was behind the dugout several rows up. If you want bleacher seats, it's rarely a problem because the Orioles play in the fourth largest stadium in the Grapefruit League. Just be aware that the left field bleachers are not open for every game, and the stadium can sell out. When the Red Sox come to play the Orioles it's standing room only.

Whoever they're playing, if you want the best seats — the seats in the lower level with the extra legroom — call ahead for a ticket order form. These seats are located only in the box seat section and they go quickly.

As for prices, this is one of the most reasonable ballparks in the Grapefruit League. The box seats with the great legroom are among the less expensive top tickets in Spring Training. Parents will appreciate the special $5 general admission price for kids 3 to 14 — the lowest priced ticket in Spring Training. Kids under 3 get in free if they sit on their parent's lap. Seniors (60+) can get Reserved Grandstand tickets for half price for weekday afternoon games if they buy them before game day.

Capacity: 8,340
Average Attendance: 5,729
Ticket Prices:
   Box Seat $20
   Reserved Grandstand $14
   General Admission, Adults $10
   General Admission, Children (14 and under) $5
For Tickets: 954-776-1921

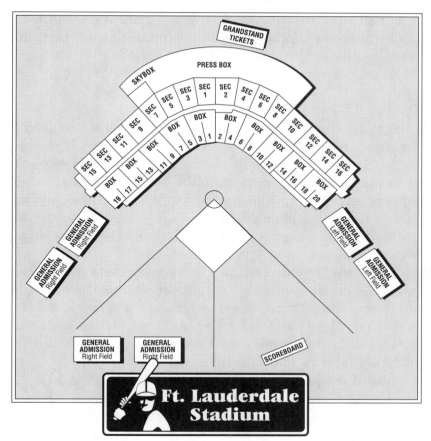

Programs

If you're an Orioles fan, you should buy a program. If not, don't bother. The Orioles program is actually a Spring Training version of the Orioles newspaper, "Outside Pitch." It has little coverage of Spring Training other than a story on the team's season outlook and an insert with the team's roster and invitees — which is not updated as Spring Training progresses.

The program has an alphabetical roster, but not a numerical one, and there are no individual pictures of the players. So during pre-game warm-ups, it's hard to use the program to identify players. To make things worse, the program is on newsprint. On a hot, sweaty day, expect your fingers to be black after reading through it. Perhaps the newsprint is an intentional follow through on the antique feel of the park.

Finally, the program carries advertisements from Baltimore, not Fort Lauderdale. The only local information — and there isn't much — is on a four-page insert, which includes a scorecard.

Cost: Program plus scorecard $4, Scorecard alone $1

Seats

Fort Lauderdale Stadium has one of the most confusing stadium arrangements in the Grapefruit League. If you are in the bleachers, you can't go to the grandstands. If you're in the grandstands, you can't go to the bleachers. So figure out where you're sitting before you go to the park. A nice touch is that this is one of only a few stadiums with seating in the outfield, but you can't reach it unless you have a ticket to the right-field bleachers.

The comfort level depends on where you sit. The bleachers here, as at most stadiums, are just that, long metal seats. The seats in the reserved grandstand section are old and somewhat uncomfortable wood planks that fold up. They do, however, have armrests. The box seats are another story. They may be the best seats in all of Spring Training thanks to their generous legroom.

One of the most frustrating things about sports today is the lack of space between the seats. Throughout most games, you're standing up to let people in or out, or you're bumping into people to get to your own seats. In Fort Lauderdale Stadium's box seat section, that is never a problem. You have almost two to three feet between seats, leaving plenty of room to stretch out or walk the aisles. What a difference!

Shade

There are plenty of seats in the shade at Fort Lauderdale Stadium. In fact, you're going to have to hunt to find seats in the sun, thanks to the way the seats face and the stadium's roof. First, the seats face the northeast. During Spring Training, the sun is in the southern sky, meaning the sun is to your back here. Second, there is a large roof that stretches over the entire reserved grandstand section. If you want shade, you are virtually guaranteed it in the grandstands.

Those who want the sun should aim for the general admission seats in either the right or the left field, where you will get the best sun on your face. If you sit in the box seats, your neck will burn, but your face won't.

Food & Drink

One of the best things about the Fort Lauderdale ballpark is the smell as you enter the stadium. The main entrance leads to the concession area, where on each side there are two large barbeque cookers. Most of the stadium's hot dogs and burgers are cooked right here, which makes them tastier than most. The cheeseburgers are especially good — thick and juicy.

While the food selection is limited, it includes tasty slushies, milkshakes, and soft ice cream served in miniature baseball helmets. There is a long line for the single ice cream stand.

Note: In many stadiums, you can buy a bottle of water and then refill it at the water faucets. When I've done that here, the water from the faucet was always a light tan color. However, management tells me that problem will be fixed before the first ball is tossed out in Spring Training 2007. You may want to give it a try before investing in several bottles of water.

Souvenirs

Where you get your souvenir will depend on where you're seated. Head for the main entrance if your seats are in the boxes or reserved grandstands. You'll find a stand on each side of the entrance. Both are small and all the souvenirs are behind the counter. If you have general admission seats, you'll be shopping from a covered cart that serves your seating area.

Wherever you shop, expect to choose from a small selection. You'll find little but the usual t-shirts, hats, and knickknacks. The only thing I saw here that I didn't find at other parks was a Baltimore Orioles infant hat.

Autographs

Your chances of getting an autograph depend on where you're sitting and how early you come. Because the players enter and exit the field through the dugout here, it's tough to get autographs after batting practice. So come early for batting practice if you want an autograph. The gates open two hours before gametime.

If you're seated in the main seating bowl (boxes or reserved grandstand), you'll have to get autographs right by the dugout. While the area is small, players are close enough to the stands here that they are quick to come over to sign. There is one road-block. The owner's box is closest to the dugout and the guard will not let you in there; so you just have to get as close as you can.

If you are sitting in the right field bleachers, you can some-times pick up an autograph at the infield corner of the fence. While many of the stars will not come over, you will get some players.

If you are in the left field bleachers, you can forget about getting any Orioles' autographs. You'll be nowhere near them (they work out on the right field side) and the stadium's de-sign prevents you from walking over to the grandstands or the right field bleachers.

You can also stand next to the chain link fence surrounding the players' parking lot. It's guarded and you can't get in. But some players will come over if you call to them by name, and others will stop to sign in their cars.

A Game or an Experience?

Fort Lauderdale Stadium is built for the true blue baseball fan. There is nothing to do here but watch the warm-up and the game. There's no playground, no entertainment, no music. Just baseball, which is OK for some people.

Up Close & Personal?

One of the best features of Fort Lauderdale Stadium is the proximity of the grandstand seats to the playing diamond. Sit in the box seats behind home plate or the dugout and you're almost on top of the players. The stadium is small as well, meaning there really isn't a bad seat in the grandstands. Even at the top of the park, you're still pretty close to the players.

The bleachers are another story. They are so far from the outfield lines that you'll need binoculars.

Getting Away

The road system around the park is not the greatest. A two-lane road connects the parking lots to the four-lane road that goes to the highway. On busy days, this will get crowded.

That said, it's a pretty quick drive to the Interstate or Florida's Turnpike once you hit the highways.

Before & After the Game: Restaurants

Restaurants within easy reach of the stadium include:
- Riggins Crabhouse, I-95 Exit 61, 607 Ridge Road, Lantana; 561-586-3000
- Starlite Diner, 6201 North Andrews Avenue, Fort Lauderdale; 954-938-1116
- Hooters of Cypress Creek, 6345 North Andrews Avenue, Fort Lauderdale; 954-928-0026
- Sweet Tomatoes, 6245 North Andrews Avenue, Fort Lauderdale; 954-771-7111
- Champps Restaurant & Bar, 6401 North Andrews Avenue, Fort Lauderdale; 954-491-9335
- Carlucci's Italian Ristorante 6351 North Andrews Avenue, Fort Lauderdale; 954-493-8600

Before & After the Game: Attractions

For more attractions and activities, check the Greater Fort Lauderdale Convention & Visitors Bureau web site, www.sunny.org.
- Boomers!, 1700 Northwest First Street, Dania; 954-921-2416; www.boomersparks.com
  Hours: Sunday to Thursday 10:00 a.m. to 12:00 a.m., Friday to Saturday until 2:00 a.m.
  Admission: None. You pay by the ride or activity.
  Come here for a range of activities, from go-karts, Naskart racing, and bumper cars and boats to arcade games, miniature golf, rock-wall climbing, and batting cages.
  Price: Prices range from $1 for 18 pitches in the batting cage up to $15 for Sky Coaster. A round of miniature golf costs $6.
- Dania Beach Hurricane, 1760 Northwest First Street, Dania; 954-921-RIDE
  Hours: Sunday to Thursday 10:00 a.m. to 11:00 p.m., Friday to Saturday until 2:00 a.m.
  Admission: Unlimited rides for $12
  South Florida's only wooden roller coaster offers

3,200 feet worth of adrenaline-pumping excitement and speeds up to 55 miles per hour. The ride lasts two minutes.

- Discovery Cruise Line, Cruise Terminal 4, Port Everglades, Fort Lauderdale; 800-937-4477, 305-597-0336; www.discoverycruise.com
  Hours: Sails daily at 7:45 a.m., returns at 10:00 p.m.
  Price: $125 per person Monday through Thursday, $145 Friday through Sunday, not including various taxes, gratuities, and service charges.
  Take a one-day cruise to Freeport, Grand Bahama Island. The price includes three buffet meals onboard (breakfast and lunch on the way to Freeport and dinner on the way back), plus shows, a disco, swimming pools, and deck chairs. Like most cruise ships these days, this one is equipped with a casino. You get into Freeport at 1:00 p.m. and leave at 4:45 p.m. Cruise 'N Stay vacation packages are also available.
- GameWorks, Sawgrass Mills Oasis, 2608 Sawgrass Mills Circle, Sunrise; 954-845-8740, www.gameworks.com
  Hours: Sunday to Thursday 11:00 a.m. to midnight, Friday and Saturday 11:00 a.m. to 2:00 a.m.
  Admission: None. You pay to play.
  GameWorks is 20,000 square feet of state-of-the-art video games. Plus a full bar and the GameWorks Grill, a full service restaurant. Game cards start at $7.
- Hollywood Classic Casino, 4150 North State Route 7, Hollywood; 888-222-7466, 954-961-3220
  Hours: Daily from 11:00 a.m. Poker casino open 24 hours.
  Prices: $22, $33, and $44 packages
  The first casino built on a reservation, Hollywood Seminole Gaming offers prize money up to $200,000 and poker tournaments two to three days per week (Sunday and Wednesday as we go to press).
- Museum of Discovery & Science and Blockbuster 3-D IMAX Theater, 401 Southwest Second Street, Fort Lauderdale; 954-467-6637, www.mods.org
  Hours: Monday to Saturday 10:00 a.m. to 5:00 p.m.,

Sunday noon to 6:00 p.m.
Admission: Adults $14, Seniors $13, Children (3 to 12) $12
You'll find over 200 hands-on exhibits and a five-story IMAX theater here. Admission includes all exhibits and one IMAX film.

- Sawgrass Mills Mall, 12801 West Sunrise Boulevard, Sunrise; 954-846-2300, www.sawgrassmillsmall.com
Hours: Monday to Saturday 10:00 a.m. to 9:30 p.m., Sunday 11:00 a.m. to 8:00 p.m. for the shops; the Oasis is open till the wee hours.
Florida's largest retail and entertainment mall features 400 name-brand stores and outlets, along with the Oasis, a hub for restaurants, bars, and entertainment, including a 23-screen movie multiplex. The mall is 10 miles west of Fort Lauderdale.

Before & After the Game: Activities

Golf

- Colony West Country Club, 6800 North Pine Island Road, Tamarac; 954-726-8430
- Deer Creek Golf Club, 2801 Country Club Boulevard, Deerfield Beach; 954-421-5550
- Emerald Hills Golf Club, 4100 North Hills Drive, Hollywood; 954-961-4000
- Jacaranda Golf Club, 9200 West Broward Boulevard, Plantation; 954-472-5836
- TPC at Heron Bay, 11801 Heron Bay Boulevard, Coral Springs; 954-796-2000

Fishing

- Action Sportfishing, Fort Lauderdale; 954-423-8700
- All-Inclusive Sportfishing, Fort Lauderdale; 954-803-1135
- Fish Lauderdale, Fort Lauderdale; 888-484-FISH
- New Latitude Sportfishing, Fort Lauderdale; 954-907-0967

Hotels Near the Ballpark

- Sheraton Suites at Cypress Creek, 555 Northwest 62nd Street, Fort Lauderdale; 954-772-5400
- La Quinta Inn, 999 West Cypress Creek Road, Fort Lauderdale; 954-491-7666
- Westin Fort Lauderdale, 400 Corporate Drive, Fort Lauderdale; 954-772-1331
- Courtyard Marriott on Cypress Creek, 2440 West Cypress Creek Road, Fort Lauderdale; 954-772-7770
- Marriott North Fort Lauderdale, 6650 North Andrews Avenue, Fort Lauderdale; 954-771-0440
- Extended Stay America – Fort Lauderdale, 5851 North Andrews Avenue, Fort Lauderdale; 954-776-9447

Chapter 4

Boston Red Sox
City of Palms Park

Fort Myers

As I sat in my hotel room in Fort Lauderdale, I was worried. A consistent procrastinator, I had waited to buy tickets until two days before the Boston Red Sox game against the Cleveland Indians across the peninsula in Fort Myers. After wading through the lengthy voice mail system, the results came through: There weren't any tickets!

This is a scary situation for anyone on vacation who wants to see a show or a sporting event. What happens if the only day you've planned for a ballgame, the game is sold out? You have to rearrange your schedule or miss the event.

I quickly rearranged our schedule. Instead of spending the next day relaxing in Fort Lauderdale as planned, we would have to get up early, drive across the state, and get standing room tickets to that day's Red Sox/Pirates game. Only then could we see the Red Sox play in their home stadium. It was not exactly the way to get my wife to fall in love with Spring Training.

The moral of this story is get your tickets early if you plan to go to a Spring Training game in Fort Myers. There just aren't that many to go around. There are only two ballparks within fifty miles and both are relatively small. Besides, the Red Sox are a hot team. (Fort Myers is one of the only places you'll have this problem.)

That said, going to a ballgame in Fort Myers is a wonderful experience. City of Palms Park is a great place to watch a game. This is one park where you can really meet most of the

Photo by Brita Meng Outzen.

stars, and there is plenty to do before and after the game.

City of Palms Park is one of the newer parks in the League. Like many of the others, it has an off-white paint job with bluish-green seats and not a lot of memorable features. Yet its overall design makes it stand above many of the newer stadiums, though not quite at the top. As you walk to the stadium from the parking lot, there is a nice wide-open area. You'll also notice dozens upon dozens of palm trees lining the walks. Even Florida residents who have a few in their yard will notice all the palms. Inside, you'll see even more of them. No doubt about it, City of Palms Park lives up to its name.

Once you step inside, you lose the open feeling. The main concourse is mostly covered and walls or large fences line both sides. However, the congested dark concourse is made up for when you walk inside the grandstands and see that the top row is not all that far from the field. You will feel intimately connected with the players and the game here.

There's lots of shade thanks to a large roof, and lots of little nooks and crannies to explore. While the park is limited in its souvenir and food selections, there are enough of both to satisfy most visitors.

The one truly memorable spot here is a walkway at the top end of the left field bleachers. From it you can watch the Red

Sox players interact with their children, wives, parents, and friends in a courtyard area below. At one game I attended, I watched Pedro Martinez relax and talk with friends for about thirty minutes, while two of his children chased each other through the batting cages. It was a great reminder of how baseball players are just like you and me.

Of course, the only reason I found the walkway was because I didn't have a seat. Perhaps there are some good things about procrastinating.

Fast Facts

City of Palms Park
2201 Edison Avenue
Fort Myers, FL 33901
877-RED-SOXX
http://boston.redsox.mlb.com

Getting There

Take I-75 to Exit 136, Colonial Boulevard. Drive west four miles to Cleveland Avenue (U.S. 41). Turn right (north) and drive about 2.5 miles to Edison Avenue. Turn right and proceed to the stadium.

Parking

City of Palms Park is very near downtown Fort Myers, but unlike most downtown parks, it has ample parking and it's very close to the stadium. You'll find the rather large lot right across the street, on the west side of the ballpark.

Cost: $7

Tickets

Buy your tickets early. This is the toughest ticket in all of Spring Training. The Red Sox averaged over 800 people more than the stadium's seating capacity at every game, meaning nearly every game was standing room only. Fortunately for last-minute planners, many of the standing room tickets are held back until game day.

Standing room tickets allow you to stand in the main aisle that separates the lower level seats from the upper level seats.

It's not a bad view, just stake your place early and don't leave it open. An alternative is to go to the top of the third base grandstands. There are picnic tables there that open up when the game starts. Pull one to the edge of the seating area and have a fine time. Yet another alternative is to head for the bleachers that run almost to the outfield on the first base side. Again, get there early if you want to sit down. There are also some grassy areas in front of the bleachers, but those go quickly, too.

Another option is to stand in the walkway above the left field seats, as I mention above. Behind this walk are the Red Sox' training areas and it's not uncommon to see the players with their families and friends, often in their street clothes. Standing here has the extra advantage of putting you close to two prime autograph areas (see below).

Capacity: 6,990
Average Attendance: 7,878
Ticket Prices:
Box Seats $24-$44
Reserved Seats $21
Bleachers $13
Lawn $12
Standing Room $10
For Tickets: 877-733-7699 or 239-334-4700

Programs

Do not forget to buy a program, especially if you are a Red Sox fan. The Red Sox put out one of the best programs in Spring Training. Why so? Because it has everything a baseball fan needs. You'll find individual photos of every player on the team and a very detailed explanation on how to keep score. The stories are in-depth and focus on Spring Training. For instance, the program had a history of the Red Sox Spring Training, a profile on every new player, and a rundown of new players who started Spring Training better than anyone expected. It also included a mini-poster for the kids, featuring six of the Red Sox current stars.

In addition, there's plenty of information about Fort Myers, albeit in the form of advertisements. Still, just about everything a visitor would want to do was advertised.

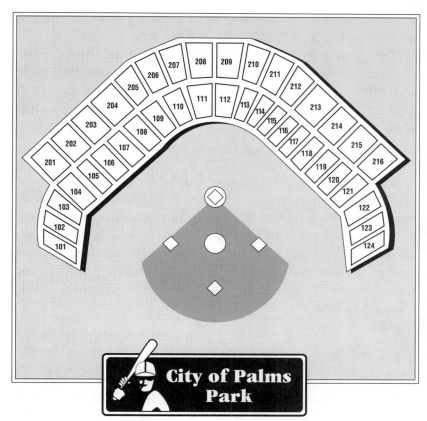

About the only thing missing was a numerical listing of the players. The Red Sox do not wear their last name on the back of their jersey, so when a player is coming by it is difficult to use the program to find out who he is.

Cost: $4

Seats

This is a ballpark where it's very easy to find your seats. There is only one concourse under the stands, and there are only a couple of entrances to the main seating aisle. Should you have any questions, you'll find plenty of ushers around to direct you.

Shade

The stadium is perfectly set up for the Florida sun. On the third base side, the seats are almost entirely in the shade. On the first base side, you get sun in either the reserved seats or the bleachers. Grab a seat close to the outfield wall on either side of the stadium and you'll also get sun.

Tip: If you do not want to run the risk of sitting in the sun (or of sitting in the sun for more than a specified time), ask when you buy your tickets if your seat is in the shade. The ticket sellers know exactly what time, if at all, each seat becomes shady.

Food & Drink

This is a weak spot at City of Palms Park. Despite the large number of people who have retired here from Boston and the many New Englanders who come here on vacation, the stadium does not serve the Red Sox' traditional Fenway Franks. Anyone who's been to Fenway Park in Boston understands how good Fenway Franks are. It's surprising they don't import them. An additional disappointment is the lack of anything unusual in terms of concession food; you'll find everything here at other parks.

Souvenirs

There have been significant improvements in City of Palms' souvenir store and stands in the past couple of years. Formerly dark, cramped, and filled mainly with Red Sox garb, the main store on the third base side appears to have doubled in space. The dark décor has been replaced with a pleasing light wood grain and the merchandise is varied and spread out. The difference it makes is astounding. While it can still get crowded and you can expect to wait in line to get in if you visit right near gametime, the shopping experience is much, much better. The selection on my most recent visit included such unusual items as a baby rattle and a bookmark.

A second stand on the first base side has been expanded as well. In past years, this was a true stand. You walked up and pointed to the item you wanted. Now, you can walk in and shop.

Autographs

This is one place where it doesn't do any good to get to the game two hours early for autographs. The Red Sox won't sign until 20 minutes before the game. Some will also sign after they are done playing.

Like many of the newer ballparks, City of Palms protects the players from autograph seekers because they enter the clubhouse from the dugout. But, unlike the players at many of those other Spring Training sites, the Red Sox go out of their way to sign autographs.

The best bet to get a superstar's autograph before the game is to wait about midway down the third base line. About 40 minutes before the game, the players come out to start warming up. About 20 minutes later, most of the players will walk over to the stands at a point about midway down the third base line and sign balls.

Later on, the place to get autographs is at the end of the third base line. After the stars are done playing, some will run the outfield wall, allowing for three prime areas to target: the grandstands at the end of the third base line, the chain link gate at the end of the main seating walkway, and beside the end of the upper grandstands. Some players will walk to the grandstands at the end of the third base line to sign. Others will stop at a chain link gate, which is down about six stairs from the main seating walkway, but is easily accessed. Finally, there is a bridge beside the end of the upper grandstands that every player must walk under to get to his car. Some will stop and sign, others won't.

A Game or an Experience?

In true New England style, this is just a game. There is little in the way of fireworks or rock music or mid-inning contests. The Red Sox fan loves his or her baseball and that's the reason they come out. For the younger kids, there is a traditional pitching game, where you guess the speed of your pitch. Other than that, you better like baseball. There is little else on offer.

Up Close & Personal?

The dugouts are reachable and the players come closer to the fans in pre-game warm-ups and after the game than they do in most other parks.

Getting Away

City of Palms Park is not an easy stadium to find without directions, but it is fairly easy to leave. There are four-lane roads heading in nearly every direction — though some of the lanes are blocked before and after the game to let pedestrians cross.

Tip: Be careful crossing the street back to the parking lot. With two of the lanes next to the park closed to cars, it's easy to feel you don't have to watch for traffic. You do!

Before & After the Game: Restaurants

- The Veranda, 2122 Second Street, Fort Myers; 239-332-2065
- Joe's Crab Shack, 2240 West First Street, Fort Myers; 239-332-1881
- French Connection Café, 2282 First Street, Fort Myers; 239-332-4443
- Morgan House, 2207 First Street, Fort Myers; 239-337-3377
- The Oasis Restaurant, 2260 Martin Luther King, Jr. Boulevard, Fort Myers; 239-334-1566
- Farmer's Market Restaurant, 2736 Edison Avenue, Fort Myers; 239-334-1687
- Pinchers Crab Shack, 13021 North Cleveland Avenue, Fort Myers; 239-652-1313

Before & After the Game: Sports Bars

- Hooters, 4411 Cleveland Avenue, Fort Myers; 239-275-4666
- Jerseys Sports Café, 13971 North Cleveland Avenue, Fort Myers; 239-995-2900
- Cigar Bar, 1502 Hendry Street, Fort Myers; 239-337-4662
- Shoeless Joe's, 13051 Bell Tower Drive, Fort Myers; 239-437-0650

Before & After the Game: Attractions

For more about things to do in the area, check Fort Myers' home county web site, www.leeislandcoast.com.

- The Big M Casino, 450 Harbor Court, Fort Myers Beach; 888-373-3521, 239-765-PLAY, www.bigmcasino.com
  Hours: Sails Tuesday to Sunday at 10:15 a.m. and 6:00 p.m.
  Cost: Morning cruise $10, Evening cruise $10, except Friday and Saturday $20
  This luxurious gaming yacht offers Las Vegas-style casino gambling on its two daily sailings from Moss Marine on Fort Myers Beach. A buffet and a la carte dining are extra. Adults only, reservations required.
- Edison-Ford Winter Estates, 2350 McGregor Boulevard, Fort Myers; 888-377-9475, 239-334-7419, www.edison-ford-estate.com
  Hours: Daily 9:00 a.m. to 5:30 p.m., last tour 4:00 p.m.
  Admission: Adults $20, Children (6 to 12) $11. (Lower price options that limit visits to certain areas are also available.)
  Tour the winter homes of Thomas Edison and his neighbor and friend Henry Ford. Tours include Edison's lab, both homes, and a museum.
- Imaginarium Hands-On Museum, 2000 Cranford Avenue, Fort Myers; 239-337-3332
  Hours: Monday to Saturday 10:00 a.m. to 5:00 p.m., Sunday noon to 5:00 p.m.
  Admission: Adults $8, Seniors (55+) $7, Children (3 to 12) $5
  Hands-on exhibits, including a hurricane simulator and fossil dig, along with aquatic exhibits such as a 550-gallon coral reef tank, a 190-gallon fresh water lagoon, and a touch tank. "Hands-On Fun Shows" at 11:00 a.m. and 2:00 p.m.
- Mike Greenwell's Family Fun Park, 35 Pine Island Road, Cape Coral; 239-574-4386
  Hours: Sunday to Thursday 10:00 a.m. to 10:00 p.m., Friday and Saturday 10:00 a.m. to 11:00 p.m.
  Admission: Free; cost of rides and activities varies
  Former Red Sox outfielder Mike Greenwell owns this amusement center. It offers a fish feeding dock, a paintball arena, miniature golf, and batting cages.

Before & After the Game: Activities

Fishing

- Back Country Fishing Charters with Captain Paul Hobby, 13371 Electron Drive, Fort Myers; 239-433-1007
- One More Cast Charters, 14869 Kimberly Lane, Fort Myers; 239-454-4934
- Captain Tony's Fishing Adventures, 18800 San Carlos Boulevard, Fort Myers Beach; 239-415-0515
- Joyce Rehr's Fly Fishing & Light Tackle Guide Service, 1155 Buttonwood Lane, Sanibel; 239-472-3308

Golf

- Gateway Golf & Country Club, 11360 Championship Drive, Fort Myers; 239-561-1010
- Shell Point Golf Club, 16401 On Par Boulevard, Fort Myers; 239-433-9790
- Beachview Golf Course, 1100 Parview Drive, Sanibel; 239-472-2626
- Gulf Harbour Yacht & Country Club, 14490 Vista River Drive, Fort Myers; 239-437-0881

Hotels Near the Ballpark

- Winyah Hotel & Suites, 2038 West First Street, Fort Myers; 239-332-2048
- Holiday Inn Select Fort Myers – Airport, 13051 Bell Tower Drive, Fort Myers; 877-617-4768, 239-482-2900
- Holiday Inn Historic District, 2431 Cleveland Avenue, Fort Myers; 239-332-3232
- Best Western Waterfront, 13021 North Cleveland Avenue, North Fort Myers; 239-997-5511

Chapter 5

Cincinnati Reds
Ed Smith Stadium

Sarasota

Leaving Ed Smith Stadium, I saw something I never thought I'd see. I waved two men across the aisle in the parking lot. They waved to say thank you. That's when I noticed these weren't your average fans. They were Pittsburgh Pirates outfielder Kenny Lofton and another player walking to their cars.

While this is typical of the surprises and experiences you'll find at Spring Training, it is not something you would expect at Ed Smith Stadium. The stadium is about as nondescript as any stadium in the Grapefruit League. A chain-link fence surrounds it and the design is pure cement. It's as if they built the stadium to match Cincinnati's Riverfront Park, the one they tore down recently.

There's little to like about Ed Smith Stadium. While it comes close in size to some of the League's intimate older parks, it's missing the things that would make it quaint. For instance, there is little to say "Wow!" about. Well, aside from the "Big Red Smokey" and the rib tips, there's nothing to say "Wow" about. And the lack of the Wow-factor hits you as you walk into the stadium and notice that there is no roof over the main concourse. Do not go to Ed Smith Stadium if there is a chance of rain. You will get wet.

The other item that hits you very quickly is the lack of large concession and souvenir stands. The main souvenir area is an outdoor stand right near the entrance, and the concession

Photo courtesy of the Cincinnati Reds.

stands are hidden in the walls of the stadium.

Other than the colors of the seats, it's a fairly typical stadium inside, with little to excite your eye. The seats in this bare concrete stadium are all blue, with some red, white and blue bunting at the back. Only the metal gates and railings are painted red. The red makes sense, of course: Ed Smith Stadium is home to the Reds. But the blue seats are very blue and seem out of place in a stadium that houses a team with no blue in its colors.

There are bleachers here, but not a lot. There is shade, but, again, not a lot. And there is little entertainment. In fact, at the game I attended the fans' excitement peaked when two Hooters waitresses passed out coupons for free chicken wings after the game. They couldn't give them out fast enough.

On the positive side, you'll have no trouble seeing all the action. The box seats are close to the diamond and the other seats aren't too far away. Better yet, there are a couple of offerings here you don't want to miss. The park does not rent seat cushions, but will allow you to bring your own. It's an excellent idea to bring cushions if you have them and it makes me wonder why more parks don't rent them.

The other don't-miss item is the food. In addition to the Cincinnati Reds' signature food item, the Big Red Smokey, you'll also find the Goetta Dog (pronounced "getta"). With peppers and onions, it's another Cincy favorite.

Independent concessionaires, who vary from year to year, sell specialties like hot roast beef sandwiches, smoked rib tips, or the "Home Wrecker," a monster hot dog with onions and peppers. It's hard to figure which to recommend. I'd suggest going with friends, ordering a representative sample, and sharing.

You'll find an imported beer stand on each side of the stadium, where you can pick up an ice-cold import served in a plastic bottle.

Many baseball fans will travel to this stadium for the chance to meet Ken Griffey Jr. Don't get your hopes up. You will be able to see the superstar, but you won't get close to him, thanks to one of the only unusual design facets of Ed Smith Stadium. While the players have to walk by the stands to get to the clubhouse, which is usually a good omen for autograph seekers, the door to the Reds' clubhouse is about 30 feet away from the stands. As Spring Training fans know, the players on most teams walk only as close to the stands as they have too. Here they don't have to walk close and can easily ignore fans' pleas for autographs. It's well known that Griffey won't come over at any point during the spring season.

In fact, there is really no good place to meet the players at Ed Smith Stadium. Well, maybe in the parking lot.

Fast Facts

Ed Smith Stadium
2700 12th Street
Sarasota, FL 34237
941-954-4464
http://cincinnati.reds.mlb.com

Getting There

Take I-75 to Exit 210, Fruitville Road. Follow it west to Tuttle Avenue. Turn right (north) onto Tuttle. The stadium is a half mile along, on your left.

Parking

Parking is no problem at Ed Smith Stadium. There's lots of space on the stadium's north and east sides. You'll find stadium entrances at the northwest and northeast corners and ticket stands at both gates. Fans can use either entrance, but the will call window is at the northwest corner. Park in the northern lot if you have to pick up tickets. Otherwise you'll be walking a distance.

Tip: If you park in the eastern lot, you might run into some of the visiting team — though not literally, one hopes. I let Kenny Lofton cross the street in front of my car.

Cost: $5

Tickets

You'll have a fairly easy time getting tickets for most games as the stadium averages just over 60 percent full. But as with other Spring Training ballparks, how far ahead you have to buy to be assured of a seat depends on what team the Reds are playing. If you're looking to see the Yankees or the Red Sox play in Sarasota, especially if those teams are coming only once during the spring, get your tickets early because the game will probably sell out.

On the flip side, if you're going to see the Reds when the Pirates are in town, you'll have no trouble getting tickets on the day of the game. That's because the Pirates play here several times a season and McKechnie Field, their Spring Training site in Bradenton, is only twenty to thirty minutes north of Ed Smith Stadium.

The best thing about this ballpark is the price. Ed Smith's top ticket, the box seat, is about as inexpensive as they come. Only Bradenton's stadium up the road has a cheaper top ticket. Moreover, Ed Smith's general admission ticket is among the lowest in Florida; there just aren't many of them to be had.

Capacity: 7,500
Average Attendance: 5,276
Ticket Prices:
> Box Seat $14
> Reserved $12
> General Admission $7
> Standing Room (if available): $5

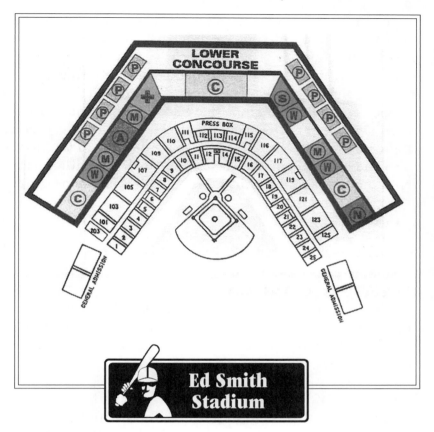

For Tickets: 941-954-4464

Programs

The Reds' program, like its admission, is reasonably priced and a worthwhile investment. It will give you everything you need to know about the Cincinnati Reds. In fact, with its insightful article about the Reds' prospects for the new season, it just might be one of the best programs in the Grapefruit League.

The program offers mug shots and fairly detailed biographies of each player on the 40-man roster. For instance, one year, I found there was enough personal information in the bios to jog my memory about Felipe Lopez. Turns out, he's the same Felipe Lopez who graduated from my wife's high school a few years ago. Without the program, I wouldn't have put the two together.

The program also includes an alphabetical roster of the team, by position, with uniform numbers. There is a statistics page, graphs, and brief instructions on how to keep score. Unlike many programs, it actually talks about Spring Training. Last time I visited, there was a lengthy article about changes in the Reds organization and some informed speculation about what fans should be looking for as the season progressed. There is also a lot of space devoted to the front office and hitting home runs. Not a big deal. But with the in-depth analysis of that article this could be the top program in Spring Training.

Cost: $4

Seats

Finding your seats is no problem at Ed Smith Stadium. There are four entrances to the reserved seating section, two near home plate and one at each end. Once inside, you'll be able to see very quickly whether you need to go right or left.

If you're heading for the bleachers, go to the main concourse and follow your eyes.

Shade

You're going to have to sit at the top of the stadium if you want shade. There is a little roof on Ed Smith Stadium, but it doesn't cover much of the stands and the stadium faces the sun for most of the game. If you sit in the left field side, bring your sunglasses. You will be facing the sun for three to four hours.

Food & Drink

This is quite simply the best thing about Ed Smith Stadium. In fact, it's some of the best food in the Grapefruit League. So bring an appetite.

Let's start with the "Big Red Smokey." While non-eaters may call it smoked sausage, the Big Red stands out from other offerings of its kind. It has just the right amount of snap, juices, and flavor. Made me wish I had bought two Smokeys and skipped the hot dog.

Another outstanding feature of Ed Smith Stadium is the

rotating roster of independent concessionaires who cook up hot specialties. One year it might be smoked rib tips, the next a monster hot dog called the "Home Wrecker." Don't miss these special treats.

The concession stands offer a selection of draft beers. While your beer will get warm quickly in the Florida sun, it's cold when it starts out. Again, Ed Smith Stadium knows how to do its concessions. Special beer stands on each side of the stadium offer upscale imports in plastic bottles.

Photo courtesy of the Cincinnati Reds.

Creating special memories for special fans is what Spring Training is all about. Here, the Reds' minor league mascot brightens a young fan's day.

Souvenirs

While Ed Smith Stadium does a great job on its food, it drops the ball when it comes to souvenirs. There are only two small souvenir venues. One is a small stand at the end of the stadium on the third base line. It's not a store, but a counter where you point to the item and the clerk gets it for you. The other is a foldout booth with a very limited selection. It's located at the front entrance to the stadium.

Still, you'll be able to get hats, bats, and baseballs, along with a few unusual items. For instance, I spotted a magnetic bobble head doll, something I didn't see anywhere else. I also noticed two road signs — a street sign and an Interstate sign — that bore the inscription, "Ed Smith Stadium."

Autographs

You're going to be hard pressed to get an autograph here. Why the problem? To start, the stadium closes all the walkways to the box seats about 30 minutes before gametime. Only ticket holders for that section can go down to the field. Then they close the aisles when the Reds enter the field to warm up. In most ballparks, this is the prime place to get autographs. The only way to avoid being shut out is to buy a box seat near the first base dugout. It's the one way you're going to get close to the players.

Catching players as they head back to the clubhouse after they finish playing is usually another good way to get autographs. Unfortunately, as I've already mentioned, Ed Smith Stadium was designed to allow the players to avoid autograph seekers, because they don't have to walk close to the stands.

Finally, for some unknown reason, the Reds seem to go out of their way to avoid autograph seekers. Ken Griffey Jr. is notorious for not signing autographs and the rest of the players seem to follow his lead.

A Game or an Experience?

For the most part, you're here to watch a game. There are a limited number of contests during the game, but nothing beyond the typical things like sticker contests.

Up Close & Personal?

You're fairly close to the players here. During warm-ups you can hear their conversations. At one game, I saw a front office employee come onto the field and ask two players to come with him. Ken Griffey Jr. started heckling them, telling them to watch out and be careful. He knew what was coming. I didn't. The next day I learned those two players were sent to the minor leagues.

Getting Away

Sarasota is a relatively easy place to get around. Even when traffic is heavy (for Sarasota) you won't get stuck. Getting to the beaches, downtown, or the Interstate takes little time.

Before & After the Game: Restaurants

- Columbia Restaurant, 411 St. Armands Circle, Sarasota (on St. Armands Key); 941-388-3987
- First Watch, two locations in Sarasota: 1395 Main Street, 941-954-1395; and 8383 South Tamiami Trail, 941-923-6754
- Cantina Latina, 3800 Tamiami Trail South, Sarasota; 941-954-1330
- The Summerhouse, 6101 Midnight Pass Road, Siesta Key; 941-349-1100
- Coasters Seafood, 1500 Stickney Point Road, Sarasota; 941-925-0300
- Sarasota Bread Company, Southgate Plaza Mall, Sarasota; 941-957-3200
- Johnny Carino's, 3005 University Parkway, Sarasota; 941-351-8883

Before & After the Game: Sports Bars

- Findaddy's, 935 North Beneva Road, Sarasota; 941-906-7795

Before & After the Game: Attractions

Newsweek magazine named Sarasota the best beach and baseball combo in Florida. The beaches are great here, but so are the other natural attractions and the shopping. Since the beaches are easy to find, we offer some suggestions for other area attractions and activities. Consult the Sarasota Convention and Visitors Bureau web site, www.sarasotafl.org, for additional ideas.

- Mote Aquarium, 1600 Ken Thompson Parkway, Sarasota; 941-388-2451
  Hours: Daily 10:00 a.m. to 5:00 p.m.
  Admission: Adults $15, Seniors (65+) $14, Children (4

to 12) $10

Exhibits here include a 135,000-gallon shark habitat, sea turtles, jellyfish, two touch pools, and manatees. Also see Mote's research in action at viewable labs.

- G.Wiz Hands-On Science Museum, 1001 Boulevard of the Arts, Sarasota; 941-309-4949

  Hours: Tuesday to Saturday 10:00 a.m. to 5:00 p.m., Friday to 8:00 p.m.

  Admission: Adults $9, Seniors $6, Children (6 to 21) $6

  Experience an array of interactive, hands-on exhibits designed for all ages.

- Sarasota Jungle Gardens, 3701 Bayshore Road, Sarasota; 941-355-5305

  Hours: Daily 9:00 a.m. to 5:00 p.m.

  Admission: Adults $12, Seniors (62+) $11, Children (3 to 12) $8

  You'll find over 70 species of animals and thousands of exotic and native plants here. Special features include a Kiddie Jungle, the Gardens of Christ, a Shell Museum, and Bird and Reptile shows, which are presented twice a day. A selection of snacks, sandwiches, and cold drinks is offered in the Flamingo Cafe. And it goes almost without saying that there's a gift shop.

- Ringling Museum of Art, 5401 Bay Shore Road, Sarasota; 941-359-5700

  Hours: Daily 10:00 a.m. to 5:30 p.m.

  Admission: Adults $15, Seniors (65+) $13, Florida Teachers and Students $5

  The 21-gallery museum is home to one of the world's most exceptional collections of Baroque art. Stroll through the historic Venetian-style Ringling Mansion, Ca d'Zan, and the delightful collection of rare circus memorabilia in the Museum of the Circus.

  Advance ticket purchase suggested. Call 941-358-3180.

- St. Armand's Circle, 300 Madison Drive, Sarasota; 941-388-1554

  Located off mainland Sarasota on Lido Key, this historic district is renowned as a cosmopolitan marketplace, complete with lush tropical plants, courtyards, and antique statuary. Over 150 upscale shops, boutiques, galleries, and fine restaurants are located here. Shop and restaurant hours vary.

Before & After the Game: Activities

- CB Saltwater Outfitters, 1249 Stickney Point Road, Sarasota; 941-349-4400
Hours: Daily 7:00 a.m. to 6:00 p.m.
Casual outdoor clothing, beach supplies, sunglasses, and snorkeling equipment are the specialties at this unique shop, which is an ORVIS Endorsed Outfitter. You can also arrange here for fishing cruises, jetski tours, boat rentals, and guide service for the bay, back-country, and inshore Gulf. Interested in new fishing equipment? There's a complete fishing tackle shop on the premises.

Fishing

- Captain Ron's Team Explorer, 2714 Datura Street, Sarasota; 941-376-2714
- Flying Fish Fleet, 2 Marina Plaza, Sarasota; 941-366-3373

Golf

- Calusa Lakes Golf Club, 1995 Calusa Lakes Boulevard, Nokomis; 941-484-8995
- Heritage Oaks Golf, 4800 Chase Oaks Drive, Sarasota; 941-926-7600
- Golf Club at Capri Isles, 849 Capri Isles Golf, Venice; 941-485-3371

Hotels Near the Ballpark

- Best Western Golden Host, 4675 North Tamiami Trail, Sarasota; 941-355-5141
- Hyatt Sarasota, 1000 Boulevard of the Arts, Sarasota; 941-953-1234
- Courtyard by Marriott, 850 University Parkway, Sarasota; 941-355-3337

- Residence Inn, 1040 University Parkway, Sarasota; 941-358-1468
- Best Western Midtown, 1425 South Tamiami Trail, Sarasota; 941-955-9841
- The Ritz-Carlton, 1111 Ritz-Carlton Drive, Sarasota; 941-309-2000

Chapter 6

Cleveland Indians
Chain of Lakes Park

Winter Haven

A big orange dome.

That's the thing I think of when I think of Chain of Lakes Park. It's the one thing that has remained constant in all my years of coming to this stadium, and I've been coming since I was a kid. Every time I drive into the parking lot, the first thing I see is that big orange dome sitting next to the entrance. And it's not even part of the ballpark. It's on a nearby building.

The dome strikes me as a symbol of this quirky old Winter Haven stadium. Over the years, Chain of Lakes Park has been added on to, moved around, and improved. Yet there's still only one entrance to the main stadium and one to the outfield bleachers. There's barely enough room to walk down the center aisle. The concession stands are in strange places and the bathrooms are round and have no doors.

And while the Cleveland Indians call the stadium home, the New England retirees, who moved nearby when the Red Sox called Winter Haven home, outnumber those from Ohio. They have only reluctantly adopted the Indians, even though the tribe has been in town for more than 10 years.

In many ways, Chain of Lakes Park is what Spring Training should be like, even though it has taken away many of the fan benefits. For instance, you want an autograph? This is one of the worst stadiums for autograph seekers. For some reason, the city planners built the right field bleachers about 10 feet off the ground. Well, most likely the reason was to

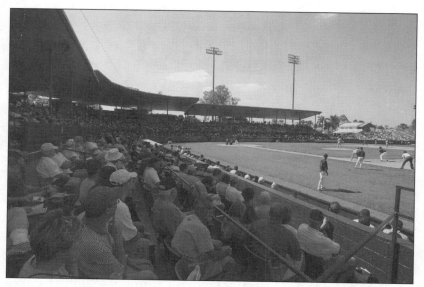

Photo by Dan Mendlik, courtesy of the Cleveland Indians.

discourage fans from asking for autographs as players walk back to the clubhouse.

Still, even though Chain of Lakes Park has adopted the no-autographs stance of many of the newer stadiums, you can tell this park is from a different era. It's intimate and the layout is just plain quirky. For instance, it's one of only a couple of parks in the Grapefruit League that has no main concourse. When you walk in to the main entrance, you'll be forced to make a decision. Go straight ahead to the bleachers, go left to the picnic area, or go right to the box seats. Or stop in the middle of the walkway first and get a Dairy Queen ice cream cone before heading to your seat. This option, of course, creates a major bottleneck. So give yourself plenty of time to get seated.

Let's say you decide to skip the ice cream and go right to your seats, which are throwbacks to older days when seats were still wide and made of wood. After sitting a minute or two, you want a drink and a hot dog. In most stadiums, you'd head back down to the main concourse, but not at Chain of Lakes Park. Here, those concession booths are sitting at the top of the stands, literally five feet behind the last row. It's a very different setup from what most of us are used to, but at least you don't miss a minute of the action when you get the urge for a hot dog in mid game.

One of the great pluses of Chain of Lakes Park is that it is a fantastic place to catch a home run ball during batting practice and during the game. The ballpark has an extensive outfield section where people hang out with their gloves in tow. There is some bleacher seating on top of a hill behind left field, but most people use this section to lie on blankets or play catch with their kids.

To get to the outfield section, buy a ticket to either the outfield bleacher or "lawn seating" sections. If your seats are anywhere else in the park, you can get into the outfield bleacher and berm areas by exiting the main entrance and going around the visiting team's buses and clubhouse into the main parking lot. Make sure you get your hand stamped so that you can get back into the stadium easily.

Whether you're watching from the outfield berm or from a seat behind home plate, at Chain of Lakes Park you're going to be treated to an old-time feel of Spring Training, the way it was played for years. Whether that's a good or a bad thing is up to you.

Fast Facts

Chain of Lakes Park
500 Cletus Allen Drive
Winter Haven, FL 33880
863-293-3900
http://cleveland.indians.mlb.com

Getting There

Take I-4 to Exit 55, U.S. 27 South. Follow it for 18 miles. Turn right on SR 540 and drive about eight miles. The park is behind the orange dome on your left just before you get to U.S. 17.

Parking

While there's only one entrance to the parking lot, it's a really big lot. If you get to the game late, you're going to be parking a long distance from the main entrance. Even if you arrive early, you're going to be walking awhile to the entrance and most of your walk will be over grass and sand.

The only exception to this is if you are seated in the outfield berm or bleachers. If that's the case, make sure you park to the left of the street as you come in. There's a separate entrance to the outfield seating, and it is within two rows of the first available parking spaces to the left of the street. (The first two rows are reserved for team and stadium staff cars.)

Cost: $5

Tickets

This is one of those parks where ticket availability depends on whether the Red Sox will be in town when you want to go. If so, plan to get your tickets as early as possible — say, when they go on sale in early January — because the game will probably sell out. Remember, the Red Sox practiced in Winter Haven for 27 years. There are still a tremendous number of Red Sox fans in the area. Games against the Yankees also tend to sell out.

You will be able to get tickets for just about any other game, however, as the park is rarely full. For instance, I attended the last home game one season, which was also the season's only night game. Both factors should have driven up attendance. But I called two days before the game and got a first row ticket directly behind home plate. I was literally three feet from the on-deck circle. On average, the stadium was just 70 percent full, in part because the outfield berm and bleachers give this antique stadium a lot more seating than you'd expect.

A word of warning about the VIP Box Seats: They are along the outfield wall. While you are closer to the field in these seats than you are in the Lower Box Seats, the VIP seats are folding chairs and you're cramped into a relatively small section. In my opinion, a Lower Box Seat, which is $8 cheaper, is the better way to go. It's not only less expensive, it's more comfortable.

Capacity: 7,000

Average Attendance: 4,631

Ticket Prices:

> VIP Box Seat $21
>
> Lower Box Seat $13

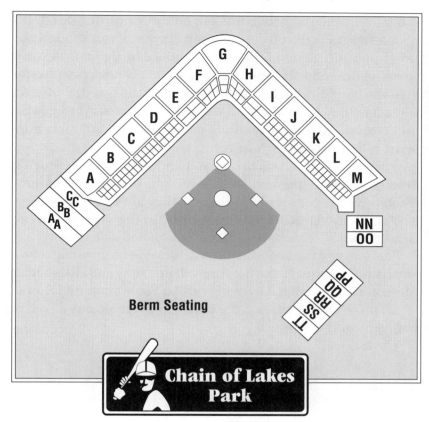

Upper Box Seat $11
Outfield Bleacher Reserved $10
Outfield Bleacher $7
Berm Seating $5
For Tickets: 863-293-3900

Program

Where are the stats? They're not in the program.

The Cleveland Indians program is a relatively thin book filled with articles, which is good and bad. It has the essential scorecard, but not an explanation of how to keep score. Today, when keeping score at a baseball game is a dying art, this should be included.

The good thing about the program is that it focuses on Spring Training. There is plenty of space devoted to the upcoming season, the new manager, new players, and so on. It's also a program devoted to Winter Haven. Even though the program is printed in Ohio, most of its advertising is devoted to companies and offerings in Winter Haven, always a plus for visitors. In addition, the program is one of the few that offers a section for children. There's a word search, a crossword puzzle, and a comic strip that reminds me of a Bazooka bubble gum strip, all aimed at the younger fan.

There is also a section to help you find your seats, although it devotes too much space to how to buy tickets. You've got to assume if someone has purchased a program, they already have tickets. The program contains the 40-man roster's mug shots, which can come in handy. A numerical roster is included as an insert.

The one glaring omission is statistics. We baseball fans love statistics. We want to see how many home runs and RBIs Victor Martinez has averaged over his career. You won't find it here.

If you're an Indians fan, the program is a must buy. If you're not, you can pass.

Cost: $5

Seats

At Chain of Lakes Park, you're going to have to depend on the ushers — or the program, if you buy one — to help you out. There are relatively few signs to point you toward your seats. The box seats are either not marked at all or are marked unclearly. In many cases, the boxes are split by an aisle. That's particularly true of the lower boxes.

Just remember, if you are seated in the outfield bleachers or berm, you need to enter through the special gate off the parking lot (see "Parking," above) not through the main entrance. If you are in the left field bleachers, use the main entrance and go straight ahead. If you're seated anyplace else, take your first right and ask the ushers for help.

Shade

This stadium is almost all shade. You're going to have to hunt for a place in the sun, but don't fret. It's available.

If you want shade, purchase any of the box seats, lower or upper, and you'll be all set. There is a large roof over the grandstands and the stadium is situated so the sun is behind you for most of the game.

If you want sun, plan on sitting in the bleachers or on the berm. In the right field bleachers, you'll get sun on your back

Photo by Dan Mendlik, courtesy of the Cleveland Indians.

The Cleveland Indians mascot, Slider, greets fans.

and on your neck. In the left field bleachers, you'll get it on your side and back. For the best sun, get a $5 seat on the berm. Then lie out on a blanket and enjoy spring in Florida. The sun will be in front of you for most of the game. You'll make everyone back home jealous.

Food & Drink

Chain of Lakes Park is not strong on concessions. However, the hot dogs snap. They come in three sizes, regular, super, and foot-long. I had the super dog and it was super — hot and juicy and thick. Just the way a hot dog should be. Make sure you shop around as the foot-long and the super dogs are available at only a couple of the stands and often not at the same one.

You'll find it hard to find anything here that's not available at any other Spring Training park. However, there are a couple of Dairy Queen stands, which you'll find only here and at Lakeland's Joker Marchant Stadium. In previous years, the stadium featured a stand for "butterfly chips," a neat cross between French fries and potato chips. However, this was gone in 2006, leaving the park with little more than typical ball park fare.

Souvenirs

The souvenir selection is actually pretty good at Chain of Lakes Park. There is a rather large souvenir store next to the ticket entrance. It sells all the traditional items, along with items you'll find only here, such as Indians Mardi Gras beads.

If you miss the souvenir store, there is a novelties stand immediately on your left as you walk into the stadium. It carries a limited selection, consisting mostly of hats, t-shirts, and Indians logo baseballs.

Autographs

Surprisingly for such an old park, this is one of the toughest places to get autographs, despite the players' willingness to sign. About the only place you're going to get an autograph is at the end of the stadium walkway on the first base side, where there is a little area about the size of a Volkswagen Bug. Every player has to pass this area to get into and out of the clubhouse. The problem is, by the time they've reached this area, they're either in a hurry to get onto the field or are already nearly back inside. So you don't have enough time to figure out which player is running by you before he's out of reach.

Two places that look like prime autograph territory are the two VIP sections. These, however, are closed to anyone who does not have a VIP-section ticket, even two hours before the game when the sections are empty. The rest of the stadium is either too high off the field to allow you to reach down to the players or simply inaccessible. Occasionally, a player will sign on the home plate side of the dugout, but you can't count on it.

Bottom line: If you plan on getting an autograph here, study up on the players so you'll recognize them instantly. Then get to the park early and stake your claim to a position along the fence at the end of the stadium on the first base side. Have hope. The few stars that Cleveland still has on its roster are eager and willing to sign autographs if you call to them.

Chain of Lakes Park does have one bonus for autograph seekers who know their baseball history. Hall of Fame pitcher Bob Feller signs autographs every game in the picnic area. He'll sign baseballs for free, but you are encouraged to buy a picture of him from the 1930s to sign. A photo costs $5 and it's worth it to meet the legend.

If you want his autograph, make sure you start waiting by the picnic tables before they announce that he's heading there. Feller signs only a limited number of autographs per game and the wait can be long. The person sitting behind me in the stands was in line for most of the game when he got his. My wait was about an inning and a half.

When I got to him, I asked Feller about his favorite Spring Training memory. He said it was going back to the hotel room after the games and studying so he could graduate high school. Remember, Feller was in the Major Leagues before he graduated. He was just 17 when he turned pro in 1935.

A Game or an Experience?

Getting to see Bob Feller should be a thrill for any baseball fan. Otherwise, seeing a game at Chain of Lakes Park is very much like seeing a game in any small town. There are sticker contests with plenty of giveaways, based on finding a sticker in your program. Almost every inning offered some giveaway the night I went.

They also had a 50-50 for a local softball team that night. This is a raffle in which the winning ticket holder splits the proceeds with the designated beneficiary. The night I was there, the winner took home over $1,200. Sadly, it wasn't me.

Up Close & Personal?

In most seats here, you're close enough to the players when they are on the field to feel like you are part of the game. The back row of seats is pretty high, however, compared with those in most other Spring Training parks. If you want to be really close to the action, sit in the VIP box seats. These put you at the field level, close to either first or third base. Another option is to buy a lower box seat behind home plate. There you will see players up close as they prepare in the batter's box.

Getting Away

A major highway runs by the stadium, allowing big crowds to exit quickly. There are only a few ways out of the parking lot, which can cause some traffic backups. But even allowing for these delays, you should be on the road in 10 to 15 minutes.

Before & After the Game: Restaurants

- Christy's Sundown Restaurant, 1100 Third Street Southwest, Winter Haven; 863-293-0069
- Chili's Bar & Grill, 699 Cypress Gardens Boulevard, Winter Haven; 863-299-9555
- Outback Steakhouse, 170 Cypress Gardens Boulevard Southeast, Winter Haven; 863-295-9800
- Applebee's, 201 Cypress Gardens Boulevard, Winter Haven; 863-294-7777

- Andy's Drive-In Restaurant & Igloo, 703 Third Street Southwest, Winter Haven; 863-293-0019
- Shells Seafood Restaurant, 1551 Third Street Southwest, Winter Haven; 863-299-7393

Before & After the Game: Sports Bars

- Beef 'O'Brady's Family Sports Pub, 300 Cypress Gardens Boulevard Southeast, Winter Haven; 863-293-9464
- All Star Grill North, 906 Spring Lake Square, Winter Haven; 863-299-7030

Before & After the Game: Attractions

While Winter Haven is just a short distance from the theme parks in Orlando, there is plenty to do in Polk County, the spring home of the Indians. You'll find the county convention and visitors bureau web site at http://www.sunsational.org.

Note: The list of attractions here is the same as in *Chapter 7*, but the restaurants, sports bars, and hotels are different.

- Cypress Gardens, 6000 Cypress Gardens Boulevard, Winter Haven; 863-324-2111, www.cypressgardens.com
  Hours: Daily 10:00 a.m. to 6:00 p.m. (in March)
  Prices: Adults $39.95, Seniors (55+) and Children (3 to 9) $34.95
  Cypress Gardens, home to lush tropical gardens, pretty Southern Belles, and acrobatic water ski shows, was Florida's original theme park. It closed in 2003, but has been revived as an all-round amusement park, complete with roller coasters. It also features live musical performances, the water ski shows that made the original park famous, and lush, walk-through botanical gardens.
- Historic Bok Sanctuary, 1151 Tower Boulevard, Lake Wales; 863-676-1408, www.boksanctuary.org
  Hours: Daily 8:00 a.m. to 6:00 p.m.
  Admission: Adults $10; Children (5 to 12) $3
  Bok Tower, a National Historic monument, is a tall, beautifully crafted Art Deco carillon surrounded by elaborate gardens and acres of longleaf pine forest. Edward W. Bok, a Dutch immigrant who made his

fortune here, commissioned the tower as his gift to the American people. You can hear a 45-minute open-air carillon concert here every afternoon at 1:00 p.m. and 3:00 p.m. (included in the admission).

- The National Historic District of Lakes Wales, Florida Located in downtown Lake Wales, the district features a variety of galleries full of art and antiques, along with beautiful architecture and a series of lovely murals relating the history of the area. Top-rated restaurants offer the ultimate in Florida dining and, after dark, offer music for listening and dancing.
- Fantasy of Flight, 1400 Broadway Boulevard Southeast, Polk City; 863-984-3500, www.fantasyofflight.com
  Hours: Daily 10:00 a.m. to 5:00 p.m.
  Admission: Adults $26.95, Seniors (55+) $24.95, Children (6 to 15) $13.95
  This place offers incredibly realistic "immersion experiences" that take you through the history of flight. You'll even get to experience a World War II bombing run in a real B-17 bomber. Afterwards, you can visit a hangar full of vintage aircraft and fly sorties in one of eight flight simulators (no extra charge). Come in the afternoon to see one of the vintage aircraft taken aloft and put through its paces.
- Explorations V Children's Museum, 109 North Kentucky Avenue, Lakeland; 863-687-3869, www.explorationsv.com
  Hours: Monday to Saturday 9:00 a.m. to 5:30 p.m.
  Admission: $5 general admission, Children under 2 free
  This downtown kids' museum features a child-sized grocery store, news station, doctor's office, bank, and more.
- Frank Lloyd Wright Buildings at Florida Southern College, 111 Lake Hollingsworth Drive, Lakeland; 863-680-4110; www.flsouthern.edu/fllwctr
  Hours: Grounds open 24 hours a day; Visitor Center Monday to Friday 10:00 a.m. to 4:00 p.m., Saturday 10:00 a.m. to 2:00 p.m., Sunday 2:00 p.m. to 4:00 p.m.
  Admission: Free

Wright designed 12 of this liberal arts college's buildings, including the planetarium. Brochures for a self-guided walking tour can be found in a clear plastic box in the parking lot between the Admissions and Administration Buildings. Look for the red and white sign. The Visitor Center contains a small collection of furniture, photos, drawings, and small gifts related to the Wright buildings.

Before & After the Game: Activities

- Florida Skydiving Center, 440 South Airport Road, Lake Wales; 863-678-1003.
  Hours: Daily 8:00 a.m. to sunset
  Price: Starts at $179
  Offers skydiving thrills for novices and experts alike.
- Westgate River Ranch, 3600 River Ranch Boulevard, River Ranch; 866-499-9077
  Hours: Varies by activity
  Price: Varies by activity
  A luxury dude ranch with horses, airboats, fishing, skeet shooting, and a Western-style saloon.

Golf

- Willowbrook Golf Course, State Road 544, Winter Haven; 863-291-5899
- Oakwood Golf Club; 3301 Old Wailes Road, Lake Wales; 863-676-8558
- Lekarica Hills, 1650 South Highland Park Drive, Lake Wales; 863-679-9478
- Big Cypress Golf & Country Club, 10000 U.S. Highway 98 North, Lakeland; 863-859-6871

Hotels Near the Ballpark

- Best Western Admiral's Inn, 5665 Cypress Gardens Boulevard, Winter Haven; 863-324-5950
- Hampton Inn, 202 Cypress Gardens Boulevard, Winter Haven; 863-299-9251
- Holiday Inn Winter Haven, 1150 Third Street Southwest, Winter Haven; 863-294-4451

- Lake Roy Beach Inn & Suites, 1823 Cypress Gardens Boulevard, Winter Haven; 863-324-6320
- Ranch House Motor Inn International, 1911 Cypress Gardens Boulevard, Winter Haven; 863-324-5994
- Howard Johnson, 1300 Third Street Southwest, Winter Haven; 800-654-2000 or 800-446-4656

Chapter 7

Detroit Tigers
Joker Marchant Stadium
Lakeland

You'll fall in love walking up to Joker Marchant Stadium. It's one of the most beautiful ballparks in the Grapefruit League. The 2002 renovations to this 40-year-old stadium are good, very good. And those renovations aren't just pleasing to the eye; they are pleasing to the soul of Spring Training because they have enabled Lakeland and the Detroit Tigers to continue a great March tradition.

Across the state, teams have moved from one stadium to the next in hopes of garnering the best financial deal. But not in Lakeland. For over 70 years now, the Detroit Tigers have come here to prepare for the season. Their history — the longest team-host city association in Spring Training — has created long-term fans, many of whom have never seen the Tigers play in Detroit.

That said, the renovations have also taken away some benefits of Spring Training that fans treasure, particularly access to the players. This is probably the second hardest place to get an autograph in the Grapefruit League. In addition, the bullpens are now in the outfield, preventing two of the joys of spring: watching the relievers warm up before they enter the game and hearing the pop of fastballs and the discussions about coaching strategies. Of course, you can still see the relievers warming up, but just barely. There's a lot of field between you and them.

Still, the renovated stadium has great appeal for several reasons. It has probably the best berm seating in the Grape-

Photo by Ryan Black, courtesy of the Detroit Tigers.

fruit League. Over the left field wall is one of the largest expanses of grassy knolls in the League. You're close enough to the outfielders that they can hear you and you them. This gives you a great opportunity to catch balls — one of the best in all of baseball. In fact, many people go to batting practice at Joker Marchant Stadium just to load up on baseballs. One man I saw had over a dozen he had caught from Tigers players.

In addition, you're really on top of the players when you sit in the lower boxes, especially on the left field side. The players and coaches are within talking distance while they are on the field and during warm-ups.

But if you sit on the right field line, which is the home team side, you're going to be surprised. This is the only park in the Grapefruit League where the protective net goes beyond the dugout. (In most Grapefruit and Major League stadiums, the net is just around home plate.) Ostensibly, the reason is to protect the fans. But the net is glaring and obstructive. It prevents fans from getting close to the players and asking for autographs. Ironically, the only time I saw a bat go into the stands during my entire tour of the Grapefruit League stadiums was here in Lakeland. It went in on the first base side, over the dugout. That's the only place where there wasn't a screen.

Other than the net and those faraway bullpens, there is little not to like about Joker Marchant Stadium. It's attractive, it's comfortable, and it has many amenities. For instance, there is a large picnic area behind the clubhouse. From it, you'll be able to see players entering and leaving the stadium. The concession stands also offer large sandwiches and subs you're not going to find at other ballparks.

When you go to Joker Marchant, sit back on the third base side or the outfield berm and chow down on some peanuts. It's an experience not to be missed.

Fast Facts

Joker Marchant Stadium
2301 Lakeland Hills Boulevard
Lakeland, FL 33805
813-686-8075
http://detroit.tigers.mlb.com

Getting There

Take I-4 to Exit 33 and follow the signs to SR 33 South. Proceed south about 2.5 miles to the stadium.

If you are on U.S. 98, the stadium is about three miles south of the I-4 overpass. From U.S. 98, turn east onto Oconee Street (SR 582). Go one block and turn left onto SR 33.

Parking

There is plenty of parking here. It surrounds the south and west sides of the stadium, and it's paved — a rare treat in the Grapefruit League. But it can be quite a walk to the stadium from your car. People get to the park very early at Lakeland. If you arrive only a couple of hours before gametime, you'll have a hike to the entrance. Allow about 15 minutes walking time if you have to park at the end of the lot farthest from the stadium.

Watch out when crossing the street near the stadium. The drive through the cones into the parking lot is confusing, so drivers aren't paying as much attention to pedestrians as they should.

Cost: $5

Tickets

Unless the Tigers are playing the Yankees or one of the other marquee teams, you'll find seats available close to game day — and maybe even then. For one thing, Joker Marchant is the third largest stadium in the Grapefruit League, with 8,500 seats. For another, the Tigers are just not the same draw as the Yankees and Braves, which play in the Grapefruit League's two largest stadiums.

That said, be forewarned. The stands here are quite high and it's easy to get a seat that is a considerable distance from the field. For instance, the left field bleachers are some of the highest metal bleachers I've ever seen. They are at least three stories tall, so watch out if you don't like heights. Then again, the berm is a great place to get a suntan and watch the game.

As for prices, overall they are about average for Spring Training parks. The top price is lower than at some places, while the general admission is one of the highest in the League.

Capacity: 8,500
Average Attendance: 5,254
Ticket Prices:
    Field Box $16 (premium games $18)
    Regular Box $15 ($17)
    Reserved $13 ($15)
    Wheelchair Accessible $13 ($15)
    Left Field Reserved $12
    General Admission $9
    Outfield Berm Seating $7
For Tickets: 813-287-8844

Programs

Joker Marchant Stadium is one of a handful of parks that doesn't have programs for sale. You can get a scorecard with a roster, but nothing else.

Cost: $2

Seats

You're not going to get lost at Joker Marchant. The ease with which you can find your seats is one of the best things about this stadium.

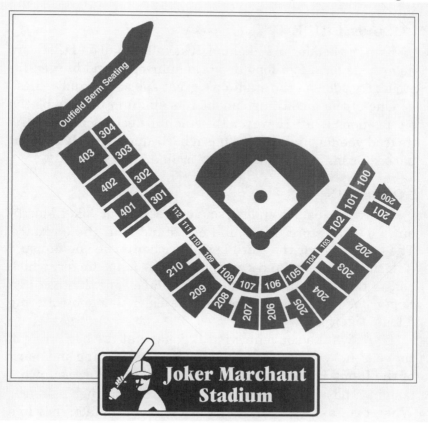

There are plenty of access points to take you from the main concourse to the seating areas. There's also a lot of signage to help you find your way. The only thing that might be confusing is the variety of ticket types.

Shade

This is one park where you are just going to have to bear the sun. There is a little roof at the top of the stadium, but not enough to provide much relief. Besides, the seats it shades are pretty high up. However, because the stadium faces north and the afternoon sun is in the southern sky in March, the sun is to your back or behind the stadium as the game winds down. Of course, you can always lie on the expansive berm, where you are at the perfect angle to soak up the rays, if that is what you are looking for.

Food & Drink

Skip the hot dog in Lakeland. It's really small and there are no options for a foot-long dog or a quarter-pound burger. Instead, try some of the stadium's great subs and sandwiches.

One of the nice things about this stadium used to be the old-fashioned fare. However, the stadium decided not to renew its food vendor, and instead has a barbeque stand. It's decent barbeque, but nothing out of the ordinary.

Souvenirs

There are just a couple of souvenir stands at Joker Marchant, no large store. You'll find one stand near the entrance. The other is near the third base bleachers. The one unusual item here is Lakeland's version of the foam finger, which boasts that the stadium's team is number one. Instead of a finger, Joker Marchant supports the Tiger theme by offering a foam tiger paw.

If you want a souvenir, visit Lakeland at the beginning of the season. I went on the last day of Spring Training and many of the items I was looking for were sold out. For instance, I bought a baseball with a team logo at every other ballpark. When I got to Lakeland, they were sold out. In fact, they had no baseballs whatsoever to sell. I had to go out to the berm before the game and buy one off of one of the guys who had caught a bunch during morning practice.

There was a silent auction of Tiger autographs and memorabilia the day I went. It took place near the main entrance and had a few decent items. If you are a Tigers fan, you should check to see if they'll be having an auction while you're there.

Autographs

The Tigers need all the fan support they can get. So it's surprising there are so few places to get an autograph here. In fact, you're going to be out of luck in many cases. Once you're inside the stadium, the only place to get an autograph from a Tiger is in front of sections 100 and 101, and that is not easy to do. If you sit on the first base side, the net that stretches from the end of the dugout to the middle of section 101 will prevent you from getting autographs there.

Bottom line: If you want to get an autograph, get to the stadium about four hours before gametime. The practice fields are to the east of the stadium and are open to the public. Players are much more responsive to requests for autographs when they are on the practice fields.

A Game or an Experience?

Because of the long baseball tradition in the area, going to a Lakeland game is an experience. Remember, the Tigers have been playing here since 1934, making them more connected to their host area than any other team in the Grapefruit League.

It's hard to tell that from looking at the ballpark, however. Joker Marchant Stadium was built in the mid 1960s and, thanks to the 2002 renovation, it looks like any of the other modern stadiums in the Grapefruit League, albeit better.

There are some contests during the game, but nothing memorable. In fact, the most memorable happening at one game I attended involved some fans. Five teenagers with KENNY painted on their chests cheered for visiting outfielder Kenny Lofton. It was one of the most entertaining sights of the spring.

Up Close & Personal?

If it weren't for the darn net you could reach out and touch the players from some of the seats. It all depends on where you sit. Because the stadium is so high, you can feel like you are in a Major League stadium if you're at the top of Joker Marchant. But if you're on the lower level, you're very close to the team.

Wherever your seats, you won't get anywhere near the pitchers and catchers. In most Grapefruit League parks, the bullpen is accessible so fans can watch pitchers warm up. At Joker Marchant Stadium, the bullpens are in dead center field and there is no access to them.

If you want to see how players act before the game, go to the end of the first base line of the stadium. There are picnic tables in front of the clubhouse and often players will come and hang out at the tables before the game.

Getting Away

Once you have exited the parking lot, getting back on the road is easy. There are lots of access roads, and one of the main roads into and out of Lakeland passes right beside the stadium. But when it comes to leaving the lot, be prepared to be patient. There are just two exits from the parking lot itself, so backups can and do occur, especially if you are in the southern lot.

Before & After the Game: Restaurants

- Outback Steakhouse, 5255 South Florida Avenue, Lakeland; 863-648-1019
- Barnhill's Buffet, 5216 South Florida Avenue, Lakeland; 863-619-6365
- The Quailhouse, 6120 U.S. Highway 98 North, Lakeland; 863-858-1970
- Bedrock Café, 3120 South Florida Avenue, Lakeland; 863-619-7576
- TapaTios, 734 Memorial Boulevard East, Lakeland; 863-686-6958
- Whistle Junction Grill & Buffet, 2815 Lakeland Hills Boulevard, Lakeland; 863-688-0355
- Fred's Market, 2120 Harden Boulevard, Lakeland; 863-603-7080
- Harry's Seafood Bar and Grille, 101 North Kentucky Avenue, Lakeland; 863-686-2228

Before & After the Game: Sports Bars

- Beef'O'Brady's Family Sports Pub, 4810 South Florida Avenue, Lakeland; 863-646-7757
- Hooter's, 3437 South Florida Avenue, Lakeland; 863-644-8461
- Winners Circle, 3234 South Florida Avenue, Lakeland; 863-646-8883
- End Zone Family Sports Cafe, 6771 U.S. Highway 98 North, Lakeland; 863-858-7226
- Lucky's Sports & Oyster Bar, 4318 U.S. Highway 98 North, Lakeland; 863-859-6830

Before & After the Game: Attractions

There is plenty to do in Polk County, the spring home of the Tigers. Because it is so close to Winter Haven, the Indians Spring Training home (they are both in Polk County), you'll find most of the same attractions listed here as in the previous chapter.

However, the restaurant, sports bar, and hotel listings are different. For more on area attractions, be sure to check the Polk County Convention and Visitors Bureau web site, at www.sunsational.org.

Note: The advantage of staying in Lakeland over Winter Haven is that it is a little closer to Tampa; so the attractions near Legends Field (see Chapter 13) are within reach when you visit the Tigers.

- Explorations V Children's Museum, 109 North Kentucky Avenue, Lakeland; 863-687-3869, www.explorationsv.com
  Hours: Monday to Saturday 9:00 a.m. to 5:30 p.m.
  Admission: $5 general admission, Children under 2 free
  This downtown kids' museum, features a child-sized grocery store, news station, doctor's office, bank, and more.
- Frank Lloyd Wright Buildings at Florida Southern College, 111 Lake Hollingsworth Drive, Lakeland; 863-680-4110; www.flsouthern.edu/fllwctr
  Hours: Grounds open 24 hours a day; Visitor Center Monday to Friday 10:00 a.m. to 4:00 p.m., Saturday 10:00 a.m. to 2:00 p.m., Sunday 2:00 p.m. to 4:00 p.m.
  Admission: Free
  Famed architect Frank Lloyd Wright designed twelve of this liberal arts college's buildings, including the planetarium. Brochures for a self-guided walking tour of these unique structures can be found in a clear plastic box in the parking lot between the Admissions and Administration Buildings. Look for the red and white sign. The Visitor Center contains a small collection of furniture, photos, drawings, and small gifts related to the Wright buildings.

- Fantasy of Flight, 1400 Broadway Boulevard Southeast, Polk City; 863-984-3500,
  www.fantasyofflight.com
  Hours: Daily 10:00 a.m. to 5:00 p.m.
  Admission: Adults $26.95, Seniors (55+) $24.95, Children (6 to 15) $13.95.
  These incredibly realistic "immersion experiences" take you on a journey through the history of flight. You'll even get to experience a World War II bombing run from inside a real B-17 bomber. Afterwards, you can visit a hangar full of vintage aircraft and fly sorties in one of eight flight simulators (no extra charge). Be sure to come by during the afternoon if you want to see one of the vintage aircraft taken aloft and put through its paces.
- Cypress Gardens, 6000 Cypress Gardens Boulevard, Winter Haven; 863-324-2111,
  www.cypressgardens.com
  Hours: Daily 10:00 a.m. to 6:00 p.m. (in March)
  Prices: Adults $39.95, Seniors (55+) and Children (3 to 9) $34.95
  Cypress Gardens, home to lush tropical gardens, pretty Southern Belles, and acrobatic water ski shows, was Florida's original theme park. It closed in 2003, but it has been revived as an all-round amusement park, complete with roller coasters. It also features live musical performances, the water ski shows that made the original park famous, and lush, walk-through botanical gardens.
- Historic Bok Sanctuary, 1151 Tower Boulevard, Lake Wales; 863-676-1408, www.boksanctuary.org
  Hours: Daily 8:00 a.m. to 6:00 p.m.
  Admission: Adults $10; Children (5 to 12) $3
  Bok Tower, a National Historic monument, is a tall, beautifully crafted Art Deco carillon surrounded by elaborate gardens and acres of longleaf pine forest. Edward W. Bok, a Dutch immigrant who made his fortune here, commissioned the tower as his gift to the American people. You can hear a 45-minute open-air

carillon concert here every afternoon at 1:00 p.m. and 3:00 p.m. (included in the admission).

Before & After the Game: Activities

- Florida Skydiving Center, 440 South Airport Road, Lake Wales; 863-678-1003,
  www.floridaskydiving.com
  Hours: Daily 8:00 a.m. to sunset
  Price: Starts at $179
  Offers skydiving thrills for novices and experts alike.
- Westgate River Ranch, 3600 River Ranch Boulevard, River Ranch; 866-499-9077,
  www.westgateriverranch.com
  Hours: Varies by activity
  Price: Varies by activity
  A luxury dude ranch that includes horses, airboats, fishing, skeet shooting, and a Western-style saloon.

Golf

- Oakwood Golf Club; 3301 Old Wailes Road, Lake Wales; 863-676-8558
- Lekarica Hills, 1650 South Highland Park Drive, Lake Wales; 863-679-9478
- Big Cypress Golf & Country Club, 10000 U.S. Highway 98 North, Lakeland; 863-859-6871
- Willowbrook Golf Course, State Road 544, Winter Haven; 863-291-5899

Hotels Near the Ballpark

- La Quinta Inn & Suites, 4315 Lakeland Park Drive, Lakeland; 863-815-0606
- AmeriSuites — Lakeland Center, 525 South Orange Avenue, Lakeland; 863-413-1122
- Best Western Diplomat Inn, 3311 U.S. Highway 98 North (south of I-4), Lakeland; 863-688-7972
- Courtyard by Marriott Lakeland, 3725 Harden Boulevard, Lakeland; 863-802-9000
- Imperial Swan Hotel & Suites, 4141 South Florida Avenue, Lakeland; 863-647-3000

- Holiday Inn Lakeland Hotel and Conference Center, 3260 U.S. Highway 98 North (south of I-4), Lakeland; 863-688-8080
- Hooters Inn, 3410 U.S. 98 North (north of I-4), Lakeland; 863-858-3851
- The Terrace Hotel, 329 East Main Street, Lakeland; 863-688-0800

Chapter 8

Florida Marlins / St. Louis Cardinals Roger Dean Stadium

Jupiter

Perhaps the most memorable happening at Roger Dean Stadium for me personally was that I remembered to put on sunscreen before I went the ballpark. If I hadn't, I would have looked as red as the St. Louis Cardinals' uniforms.

While the sun beats down on most of the baseball parks in Florida, Roger Dean is probably the sunniest stadium in the Grapefruit League. There is no roof anywhere over the grandstands. For those northerners who come to Florida expecting — no, wanting — a sunburn, this is the perfect park. If you don't enjoy the pain sun exposure brings and you can't be bothered to protect yourself, it might be a wise idea to pass on a game here. But that would be a mistake. If you pass, you will miss one of the top five stadiums in the Grapefruit League.

Roger Dean Stadium offers the best of both the new and the old and is full of great surprises. Built in 1998, it is one of the newer parks in the Grapefruit League. Its architecture and construction make it look as appealing as Walt Disney World's stadium, or any other park in the League. Yet it's built with an old time feel and a wonderful intimacy. You can reach out and almost touch the players from every seat. It's unfortunate that other parks of its era did not follow its lead in capturing the essence of Spring Training.

Even walking in to Roger Dean Stadium, you can tell it is different. The walkway area is designed to look like a small

Photo courtesy of Roger Dean Stadium / Matt McKenna.

town with row houses and tree-lined streets. The ticket area is paved brick, complete with first-class landscaping.

When you enter the stadium itself, you notice the wide main concourse. You feel like you're walking through a cavern that never seems crowded. In fact, it's the one place to go to escape the sun. There are ample concession stands and a large novelty store here, and there's never a line for the bathroom. The hot dogs are wonderful. In the grandstands, you're close to the field. In fact, there's not a bad seat in the stadium as most are not more than 25 to 30 rows up. There's a small berm for people who want to sit on the grass and a picnic area for groups. The players walk by the stands on the way to the clubhouse.

There's something to be said about the atmosphere in the park, too. Maybe it's all the Midwesterners, but the players seem friendlier here, even playing with the fans. For instance, one child near the edge of the berm was wearing an Atlanta Braves hat. The St. Louis right fielder walked over to the stands and took off the kid's hat, smiling the entire time.

In addition to all that, you'll have the chance to meet one of the greats of baseball, Lou Brock, the Cardinals' greatest player. Brock is a regular at Spring Training. He comes to help the team prepare, but he's willing and eager to sign autographs and talk with the fans.

Plus, you never know who else you may run into in Jupiter. Many of Hollywood's superstars own homes or reside in this South Florida city. The day I came, I spotted actor John Goodman walking out of the bathroom as I was walking in. He signed my baseball.

If it weren't for the lack of a roof, Roger Dean Stadium would be just about the perfect ballpark. The essence of Spring Training flourishes here.

Fast Facts

Roger Dean Stadium
4751 Main Street
Jupiter, FL 33458
561-775-1818
http://florida.marlins.mlb.com
http://stlouis.cardinals.mlb.com
http://www.rogerdeanstadium.com

Getting There

Take I-95 to exit 83, Donald Ross Road. Go one mile east to South Central Boulevard. Turn left (north) and follow it to the traffic circle, where you will go halfway around the circle to come out on Main Street. The stadium is just ahead on the right.

Parking

Compared to other ballparks, the parking here is a distance from the stadium. A rather large field near the ballpark is open to fans on game day. If you get to the game late, you're going to be walking through the field to get to the ticket window, all the while dodging fire-ant mounds. The walk is not that bad once you get out of the field and start down what appear to be the tree-lined streets of a small town.

Note: The walk back to your car is shorter because, after the game, the stadium opens up a special exit near the third base side of the main concourse, which is closer to the parking lot. Be sure to look for it.

Cost: $7

Tickets

The fact that the Cardinals and Marlins share the stadium is a bonus when targeting a game in Jupiter. It means there are only one or two days in March on which there is no baseball at the stadium. Just how easily you'll get seats for a game will depend on which team is playing, and whom they're playing.

The Marlins and Cardinals not only share the stadium but play a number of their games against each other. There's a Cardinals vs. Marlins game at least once a week and sometimes twice. Because there are so many match-ups between the teams, you have an excellent chance of picking up good tickets on Cardinals vs. Marlins game days.

Just the opposite is true, of course, when either team plays a top-tier opponent. But that's not often. During the 2006 season, the Red Sox played one game in Roger Dean Stadium and the Mets played two. Predictably, the Marlins vs. Red Sox game was the hottest ticket of the Marlins' season. You will likely find tickets available for Marlins games with lesser opponents because the team practices in its home territory.

Getting tickets to Cardinals games is harder. If you want to see the Cardinals play anybody but the Marlins, you need to buy your tickets early, especially if they are playing a marquee team. The Cardinals seem to have one of the larger followings of fans, specifically fans who like to travel. On average, there were fewer than 200 tickets left by the day of the game — a bad omen for fans who like to wait until the last moment to buy tickets.

If you do come up short for a game at Roger Dean Stadium, you can buy a berm ticket or a standing room ticket, both of which are available only on the day of the game. Standing is not a bad option, as there are plenty of vantage points from which you can enjoy the game. It's just going to make you tired. The berm is actually a pretty good place to watch a game. It turns toward the right field line and situates you so that you are looking straight at home plate.

Note: There's an added plus for berm ticketholders. The bullpen is directly in front of the berm. All the home team's pitchers sit against the berm's front wall and chat with the fans during the game. However, you must have a berm ticket to go on the berm.

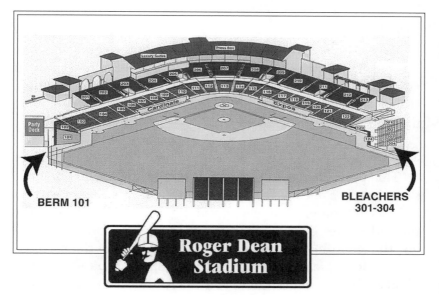

BERM 101

BLEACHERS
301-304

Roger Dean
Stadium

Capacity: 6,800
Average Attendance for Marlins Games: 4,787
Average Attendance for Cardinals Games: 6,604
Ticket Prices:
> Field Box $22 weekdays, $23 weekends
> Loge Box $20 weekdays, $21 weekends
> Bleachers $8 weekdays, $9 weekends
> Berm $8 weekdays, $9 weekends
> Standing Room $6 weekdays, $7 weekends

For Tickets: 561-775-1818

Programs

Jupiter offers a separate program for each team, complete with articles and photos of each player — a great help when you are trying to identify the players on the field. The programs also carry a section on the team's prospects from *Baseball America*. While other programs include this information on their respective teams, it is a nice touch. In addition, there are plenty of advertisements for things to do around the stadium.

The programs are not perfect. The most glaring omission is the lack of statistics for current players. Baseball is a game of statistics. Not to include them in the program is a shame.

Cost: $5

Seats

Roger Dean Stadium is a pretty easy park to find your way around. There are only two levels and one set of bleachers. If you're in the bleachers, take a left when entering the stadium. If you're on the berm, take a right. Everything here is well marked and easy to find.

Shade

This park's biggest drawback is the lack of shade; the little there is only comes part way through the game. Expect several innings in the sun wherever you sit. If you want shade, sit at the top and center sections of the grandstands. The sun will dip below the stadium during the game, shading you in the process.

Sun lovers can pick almost any seat and be assured of plenty. The bleachers allow you to sit almost facing the sun for most of the game. The first base side puts your back to the sun. The berm will let you soak up the sun all afternoon.

Food & Drink

One of the best things about this ballpark is the hot dogs. They are close to being perfect. They are big. They are juicy. They have the proper bread to meat ratio. You can't ask for more.

Well, you could ask for a better snow cone. While the line for them is quite long, the cones are unappealing. While they seem to be made in the traditional way, by pouring juice over ice chips, there is something about them that just doesn't work. Perhaps the ice chips are too big to absorb the juice properly.

Jupiter offers a wide variety of food. You'll find the Dean Dog, a jumbo hot dog with peppers and onions, a chicken nugget basket complete with French fries, and wraps. In fact, the stadium has a separate wrap stand for its health-minded fans that offers a great selection of eight different sandwich wraps.

The most unusual concession item is the Dippin' Dots. For those of you who haven't had them at one of the theme parks, these are balls of ice cream about an eighth of an inch thick. You eat a bunch of them in each spoonful. They are wonderful — a great way to cool down while sitting in the hot sun. You'll find them at a couple of other ballparks as well as here.

Souvenirs

You can pick up souvenirs at a rather large store to the left of the main entrance or at one of the souvenir stands (there's one on each side of the stadium). The main store is filled to capacity with every imaginable item from both teams. The lines are not long and you can search for a while to get your perfect souvenir without being elbowed.

There are several items here that cannot be found any other place. For instance, there is a relatively large selection of hot sauces with either the Marlins' or Cardinals' logo on the label. What hot sauces have to do with baseball is beyond me, but I know of lots of people who have quite the collection of hot sauces.

Items that make more sense are the Marlins and Cardinals hanging monkeys. In fact, after the success of the "Rally Monkey" in Anaheim, I am surprised more stadiums don't offer this item. For those not in the know, the "Rally Monkey" came out of the 2002 World Series. Some Anaheim Angels' fan started shaking a stuffed monkey whenever the team needed to rally, and it caught on.

Autographs

Autographs are not that easy to get here thanks to the layout of the stadium. It's not impossible to get them, but it's not so easy. You have to be willing to fight the crowds.

Bear in mind that the Cardinals' clubhouse is on the right side of the field and the Marlins' on the left. The best place to get Cardinals' autographs is the berm, and the number one spot is at the front of the berm. During the game, pitchers and catchers sit about a foot away from the berm. Between innings, they are more than willing to sign.

The second best place for Cardinal autographs is the right front corner of the berm as you face the field. Roger Dean Stadium is constructed so that the foul lines are away from the first base side for most of the distance. However, the berm juts toward the foul lines and every player must pass it before entering the clubhouse. Many players stop to sign here, so the people on the berm get the most autographs.

If you're seated elsewhere, a possibility is to hang out by the dugout before the game. The players are less willing to sign there than they are by the berm. But this is where Lou Brock signed my ball. You can also wait at the end of the seating aisle on the first base side. The gate leading to the clubhouse is right there and players will sometimes let you throw an item down for them to sign. It is about a 20-foot drop.

On the Marlins side, standing along the fence by the bleachers is a great place to get autographs. Other possibilities are near the dugout before the game and the end of the seating aisle on the third base side at anytime.

A Game or an Experience?

The stadium crew in Jupiter does its best to entertain. During a game I attended, the stadium had one of the best contests I have ever seen. The MC picked two people from the audience and put them on the top of the dugouts. Next, the MC played an excerpt of Jimmy Buffett's "Margaritaville," stopping it partway through. The contestants each had to sing the next line. The fans applauded to pick the winner.

Up Close & Personal?

The foul lines are far away from the stands, but the intimacy of this park reigns supreme. There really isn't a seat where you feel too far away from the action. In addition, the bullpens are literally right next to the stands, just past first and third bases. There's nothing between the fan in the stands and the players warming up. Finally, if you sit in the berm section you are literally a foot away from the players. That's as close as you'll get at any park in the Grapefruit League.

Getting Away

Give yourself a few extra minutes to get out. There are several ways to exit the lot, but all flow into two-lane roads, which wind into other roads before taking you to the highway.

Before & After the Game: Restaurants

- Thirsty Turtle Sea Grill & Market, 13981 U.S. Highway 1, Juno Beach; 561-627-8991

- Hurricane Cafe, 14050 U.S. Highway 1, Juno Beach; 561-630-2012
- Barrymore's Prime Steaks, 4050 South U.S. Highway 1, Suite 307, Jupiter; 561-625-3757
- Costello's Pizzeria and Trattoria, 1209 Main Street, Jupiter; 561-776-5448
- Masa's Sagami North, 1200 Town Center Drive, Jupiter; 561-799-6266

Before & After the Game: Sports Bars

- J.J. Muggs Stadium Grill, 1203 Town Center Drive, Unit #119, Jupiter; 561-630-9669

Before & After the Game: Attractions

While Jupiter doesn't have many activities for visitors, you will find plenty of beaches, golf courses, and other attractions within a short driving distance. For more information about them, check the Palm Beach Convention & Visitors Bureau's web site, www.palmbeachfl.com.

- Calypso Bay Waterpark, 151 Lamstein Lane, Royal Palm Beach; 561-790-6160
  Hours: Daily March to September 10:00 a.m. to 5:00 p.m., but call first. Early and late in the season, it may be open only on weekends.
  Admission: Adults $10, Children (3 to 11) $8, Children (1 to 2) $3
  An 897-foot river ride, two four-story high water slides, a children's interactive water playground, and a lap pool with two diving boards are offered here.
- Palm Beach Zoo at Dreher Park, 1301 Summit Boulevard, West Palm Beach; 561-547-WILD, www.palmbeachzoo.org
  Hours: Daily 9:00 a.m. to 5:00 p.m.
  Admission: Adults $12.95, Seniors (60+) $9.95, Children (3 to 12) $8.95
  This intimate 23-acre tropical zoological garden is home to more than 1,100 animals.
- South Florida Science Museum, 4801 Dreher Trail North, West Palm Beach; 561-832-1988, www.sfsm.org
  Hours: Monday to Friday 10:00 a.m. to 5:00 p.m., Saturday

10:00 a.m. to 6:00 p.m., Sunday noon to 6:00 p.m.
Admission: Adults $9, Seniors (62+) $7.50, Children (3 to 12) $6
An interactive hands-on science center, South Florida Museum features both permanent and traveling exhibits.

- Lion Country Safari, 2003 Lion Country Safari Road, Loxahatchee; 561-793-1084, www.lioncountrysafari.com
  Hours: Daily 9:30 a.m. to 5:30 p.m., last admission at 4:30 p.m.
  Admission: Adults $20.95, Seniors (65+) $18.95, Children (3 to 9) $16.95
  Set your own pace as you drive through seven large preserves, each with its own unique variety of wildlife.

Before & After the Game: Activities

- Loxahatchee Everglades Tours, 15490 Loxahatchee Road, Boca Raton; 561-482-6107
- Daggerwing Nature Center, 11200 Park Access Road, South County Regional Park, Boca Raton; 561-488-9953
- Rapids Water Park, 6566 North Military Trail, West Palm Beach; 561-842-8756
- Club Jet Ski / Island Waves Parasailing, 311 East Blue Heron Boulevard, Singer Island; 561-842-CLUB
- Jupiter Outdoor Center, 18095 Ocean Boulevard (A1A), Jupiter; 561-747-9666

Golf

- Breakers West, 1550 Flagler Park Way, West Palm Beach; 561-653-6320
- Delray Beach Golf Club, 2200 Highland Avenue, Delray Beach; 561-243-7380
- Emerald Dunes Golf Course, 2100 Emerald Dunes Drive, West Palm Beach; 561-687-1700
- Okeeheelee Golf Course, 7715 Forest Hill Boulevard, West Palm Beach; 561-964-4653
- The Village Golf Club, 122 Country Club Drive, Royal Palm Beach; 561-793-1400

Hotels Near the Ballpark

Most of the hotels near the ballpark are actually about 10 miles to the south in West Palm Beach. You could also stay near the beach. It is just a short drive away.

- DoubleTree Hotel – Palm Beach Gardens, 4431 PGA Boulevard, Palm Beach Gardens; 561-622-2260
- Embassy Suites Hotel – Palm Beach Gardens, 4350 PGA Boulevard, Palm Beach Gardens; 561-622-1000
- Fairfield Inn & Suites – West Palm Beach Jupiter, 6748 Indiantown Road, Jupiter; 561-748-5252
- Holiday Inn Express Juno Beach, 13950 U.S. Highway 1, Juno Beach; 561-622-4366
- Palm Beach Gardens Marriott, 4000 RCA Boulevard, Palm Beach Gardens; 561-622-8888
- PGA National Resort & Spa, 400 Avenue of the Champions, Palm Beach Gardens; 561-627-2000
- The Jupiter Beach Resort, Five North A1A, Jupiter; 561-746-2511
- Hampton Inn Juno Beach, 13801 U.S. Highway 1, Juno Beach; 561-626-9090

Photo courtesy of the Kissimmee Convention & Visitors Bureau.

At Osceola County Stadium, autograph seekers aren't just permitted, they're encouraged. Here, young fans line up at Autograph Alley for signatures from their favorite Astros players.

Chapter 9

Houston Astros
Osceola County Stadium

Kissimmee

When Osceola County announced it was putting its stadium through an $18 million renovation between the 2002 and 2003 seasons, I thought, "uh oh, they're going to make it into one of those new behemoths like the one down the road at Disney." Fortunately, they didn't. In fact, they turned Osceola County Stadium into one of the best in the Grapefruit League.

What's so great about it? It captures the essence of Spring Training. It has children's activities; it has ample spaces for autograph seekers to access the players; it has shade and sun; and it is small enough so that there is not a bad seat in the stadium. In fact, Osceola County Stadium is the smallest in the entire league. While most stadiums hold 6,500 or more, Osceola County Stadium is filled to capacity with just over 5,000 people.

It doesn't look any different from most other newer stadiums as you walk up to it. In fact, it looks pretty cookie cutter. Yes, it looks new and it has design elements that are only found on new stadiums, but its columns, metal gates, and ticket windows could be transplants from anywhere.

Once inside the main concourse, however, you start to feel the stadium is different. There is not a lot of clutter. In fact, there are only a couple of concession booths, for lemonade and programs. The rest of the concourse is wide, open-aired, and breezy.

You can really tell it is different when you walk up to the food concession stands. This is the only park in the Grapefruit League to offer a kid's meal. It comes with a hot dog, chips,

Photo by Skip Stowers Photography, courtesy of Osceola County Stadium.

and soda. It's surprising that no other park offers one because families are a big part of the crowd at Spring Training games. The souvenir stand is also different. It's not too crowded with merchandise and yet it's large enough that when there are crowds of people, you're not going to be overwhelmed.

Down the first base line, you'll see another feature you'll find only here, a playground. This seems like a no-brainer to have at a family tourist destination like a baseball field, since there are obviously very young children in attendance who could care less about baseball. The only downside is that the playground is inside a chain-link structure and some birds have moved in and built nests there. So far, management hasn't figured out how to move them out.

Watching a game at Osceola County Stadium may be one of the best experiences in the Grapefruit League. While you won't find the showboating elements that feature so prominently in the ballpark at Disney's Wide World of Sports Complex down the road, you're going to feel immersed in baseball here. This stadium is intimate. The top seat is no more than 100 feet away from the playing field.

But what makes this park really stand out is the emphasis

on providing autograph spots. While many new stadiums are designed to discourage autograph seekers, Osceola County built an entire section for them. Called Autograph Alley, it's a long wall where there are no seats. Every player must walk by it to get to the clubhouse. Of course, many players won't stop to sign, but you can certainly talk to them as they walk by. And a lot of players do stop.

Note: There are walkways on both sides of the stadium. So Astros and visiting players are both accessible to fans.

It's a shame that many baseball fans will gravitate towards the offerings at Walt Disney World, just a few miles down the road. While the Disney organization has made every effort to make sure you experience a Major League style baseball game, Osceola County has devoted its efforts to showcasing Spring Training the way baseball fans love it.

Fast Facts

Osceola County Stadium
1000 Bill Beck Boulevard
Kissimmee, FL 34744
321-697-3200
http://houston.astros.mlb.com

Getting There

Take Florida's Turnpike to Exit 244, U.S. 192, and turn west. Follow U.S. 192 to Bill Beck Boulevard and turn right. The parking lot is on the left, less than a mile from the turn.

Parking

The parking lot is right next to the stadium. It is a rather large grass field. You will not have a long walk at all if you get there early enough — an hour or two before gametime, two hours before if the visitors are a top draw. However, if you arrive at gametime, you may have a hike.

Cost: $5

Tickets

In most cases, you're going to want to get your tickets as soon as possible for games in Kissimmee. The stadium averaged over

80 percent full in 2006, which isn't all that surprising considering that Osceola Stadium is in the midst of the nation's Number One tourist destination. Remember, this is the smallest stadium in the Grapefruit League and, as such, tickets go fast.

This is especially true for games with the marquee teams. For instance, you might think that you would have a better chance of scoring Braves tickets here than at Disney's Wide World of Sports Complex down the road. You won't. And when the Yankees come to town, you're probably going to be out of luck if you didn't buy your tickets when they went on sale in January.

One of the biggest drawbacks — maybe the only drawback — to Osceola County Stadium is the lack of ticket variety. There are only two types of seats, Box Seats and Reserved. Box Seats are below the aisle and Reserved above. What that means for the fan is there are no general admission tickets, thus no cheap seats to be had. There is also no standing room. Still, the top ticket price here is one of the least expensive in Spring Training. And a $15 seat, the lower price here, is a much better value than a $20 seat at other parks. There really isn't a bad seat in the stadium.

Capacity: 5,225

Average Attendance: 4,298

Ticket Prices:
    Box Seat $18
    Reserved Seat $15

For Tickets: 321-697-3200

Programs

The program is a decent one. It focuses on Spring Training more than on the regular season, and last year's program included a history of the Astros' Spring Training seasons. It was missing some crucial details. For instance, while there are statistics from prior years for the non-invitees, there were none for the 40-man roster of regular players. That doesn't make sense. There were also no instructions on keeping score, which should be included in every program.

The program includes basic information and mug shots of players listed alphabetically. The numerical roster is only on

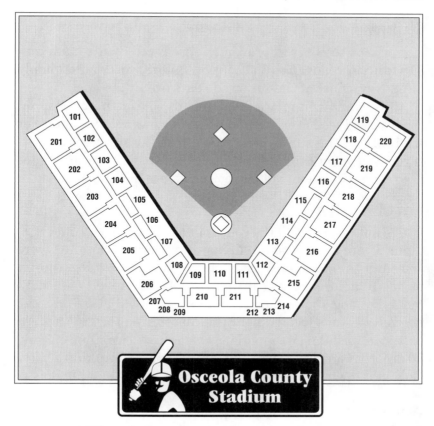

an insert. When looking up a player by number, it helps to have both in the same place.

Thankfully, the advertisements were about Kissimmee and the surrounding area. There was absolutely nothing on Houston except from the national sponsors, like Continental Airlines — a real plus in my book.

All in all, this is a decent program and an OK investment.
Cost: $3

Seats

This has to be one of the easiest places to find your seat in the Grapefruit League. There are lots of signs and only four entrances, two in the middle of the stadium and one at each end. Moreover, there are only two types of seats, Reserved, which are above the main seating aisle, and Box, which are below it.

Shade

Perhaps the best improvement produced by the stadium's $18 million renovation is the roof. Before, you would simply melt. Now, most of the reserved seats are in the shade.

If you want to be guaranteed a shady seat, sit near the top of the reserved section on the first base side toward home plate. For a mix of sun and shade, sit on the third base side near the top. If you really want to roast, sit in the box seats. The roof shades the reserved section, but the box seats are in the open.

Food & Drink

It's not hard to find the concessions at Osceola County Stadium. There are four main areas, all relatively close to where you enter the stadium. Most offer the standard hot dogs (pretty basic), hamburgers, soft drinks, and beer, as well as a kid's meal (hot dog, cookie, and a small soda). You'll also find some specialty stands located near the center area toward the first base side, including a cappuccino bar, a shaved ice stand offering 30 different flavors (more than any other stadium), and a "Cool Dog" stand, which sells ice cream in the shape of a hot dog.

Souvenirs

If you want a souvenir, you need to visit the team store. You can access it from outside the stadium next to the ticket windows. From inside, you will find it near the center of the stadium on the main concourse.

Once inside, you'll find yourself in a space with plenty of room to spare and all the traditional merchandise to choose from — hats, t-shirts, and a wide selection of baseballs among them. The one unusual item is called a "Clip Dog." Basically, it is a medium-sized stuffed animal that clips onto things. It is decked out in an Astros uniform.

Autographs

If you're an autograph collector, this is one of the top parks to visit. You'll be able to garner more autographs here than at just about any other ballpark, if the players are up to it. To get to the prime autograph area, walk to the end of the third base line. You will find a wide-open area with the team's clubhouse on one side and left field on the other. This is Autograph Alley. If you stop along the left field wall, you will get some of the lesser-known players. To get the top Astros players, walk all the way to the short fence at the end of the Alley. Wait until after the game and most players will sign for you.

For autographs from the visiting team, go to the first base side of the stadium. Here again you will find a long walkway that the visitors must pass to get from their clubhouse to the field and back. It's easy pickings if the players are willing.

Note: Unlike at many parks, getting to Osceola County Stadium early does not really improve your chances of getting autographs. Many stars won't sign until after they finish playing, and some players go to the locker room first to change and then come back out.

A Game or an Experience?

There aren't a lot of extracurricular activities here. But this is the most child-friendly park in the Grapefruit League. Don't miss the playground near the visitors' clubhouse if you're visiting with a young one.

Up Close & Personal?

There's not a bad seat in the house, mainly because it is such a small stadium. From the top row, you're only about 100 feet from the game. Plus, you can carry on conversations with players as they walk to the clubhouse. Stand along Autograph Alley and just start talking. You're only a foot or two away from where the players walk. A few seasons ago, I talked with then Astros manager Jimy Williams there.

Getting Away

While you will have a great experience in the game, you may find yourself cursing on the way out. The stadium's crew sends most drivers out of the parking lot via a long two-lane road. There is no traffic light to help drivers who want to turn left onto the main street, causing major delays for the cars behind them. Just expect to sit a while and remind yourself that this is one of the few drawbacks to Osceola County Stadium.

Before & After the Game: Restaurants
- Kissimmee Steak Co., 2047 East Irlo Bronson Memorial Highway (U.S. 192), Kissimmee; 407-847-8050
- Outback Steakhouse, 3109 West Vine Street, Kissimmee; 407-931-0033
- Roadhouse Restaurant, 4155 West Vine Street, Kissimmee; 407-932-4401
- Catfish Place, 2324 13th Street, St. Cloud; 407-892-5771
- Chevy's Fresh Mex, 2809 West Vine Street, Kissimmee; 407-847-2244

Before & After the Game: Sports Bars
- Gators, 715 East Vine Street, Kissimmee; 407-847-9595
- Beef 'O'Brady's, 2926 13th Street, St.Cloud; 407-891-1900

Before & After the Game: Attractions
You'll find more information on Kissimmee attractions and activities at the Kissimmee-St. Cloud Convention and Visitors Bureau web site, www.floridakiss.com.
- Green Meadows Farm, 1368 South Poinciana Boulevard, Kissimmee; 407-846-0770, www.greenmeadowsfarm.com

  Hours: Daily 9:30 a.m. to 4:00 p.m.

  Admission: $19 general admission, Florida residents $17, seniors (55+) $16, children 2 and under free.

  Spread over 50 acres, this petting farm conducts 2-hour guided tours ideal for small fry ages three to seven. Youngsters can meet piglets, ducklings, chicks, and other common and not-so-common farm animals, including llama, buffalo, and ostriches. Admission also covers a train ride and a trip on a haywagon.
- Old Town, 5770 West Irlo Bronson Memorial Highway (U.S. 192), Kissimmee; 407-396-4888

  Hours: Vary; generally 10:00 a.m. to 11:00 p.m.

  Admission: Free, charge for rides varies

  Old Town offers shopping, dining, and entertainment, and features over 70 specialty shops, many affordable restaurants, more than a dozen amusement park rides, 25-cent Pepsi, and the weekly "Saturday Night Cruise," a parade of 350 or so vintage automobiles.

- Gatorland, 14501 South Orange Blossom Trail, Orlando; 800-393-5297, 407-855-5496, www.gatorland.com
  Hours: Daily 9:00 a.m. to dusk (5:00 p.m. in March)
  Admission: Adults $19.95, Children (3 to 12) $12.95
  The original Orlando theme park, Gatorland bills itself as "The Alligator Capital of the World," complete with gator wrestling (man vs. gator) and opportunities to feed the gators. In March, it is also a destination for birdwatchers, who will find over 1,000 pairs of nesting herons and egrets in the trees above the park's alligator breeding marsh. These birds find the well-fed gators below to be good protection for their young from predators like raccoons and snakes. Perhaps that's why visitors can get very close to their nests without alarming them.
- Arabian Nights, 6225 West Highway 192, Kissimmee; 800-553-6116, 407-239-9223, www.arabian-nights.com
  Hours: Daily, times vary
  Admission: Adults $56.60, Seniors (55+) $37, Children (3 to 11) $31.03. Additional discounts for booking online.
  Watch beautiful horses and an engaging team of riders while savoring a prime rib (or vegetarian lasagna) meal with unlimited beverages. Horses and riders enact the tale of a princely wedding celebration with trick riding and various other equine and human acts. This dinner attraction has been voted #1 in Orlando.
- Medieval Times Dinner and Tournament, 4510 West Irlo Bronson Memorial Highway (U.S. 192), Kissimmee; 888-935-6878, 407-396-1518, www.medievaltimes.com
  Hours: Daily, times vary
  Admission: Adults $50.95 (10% discount for Seniors 55+), Children (under 12) $34.95, plus tax and tip.
  Feast on a medieval banquet while watching daring knights on beautiful horses competing in medieval tournament games, sword fighting, and jousting matches.

Before & After the Game: Outdoor Activities

- Boggy Creek Airboat Rides East, 3702 Big Bass Road, Kissimmee; 407-344-9550
  Hours: Daily 9:00 a.m. to 5:30 p.m.
  Price: Adults $21.95, Children (3 to 12) $15.95 for half-hour tours, or $45 per person for 45-minute tours.
  Experience the Central Florida Everglades on a fun and safe airboat. View local wildlife, turtles, birds, and the Florida alligator. Restaurant and gift shop. Large groups or private tours.
- Horse World Riding Stables, 3705 South Poinciana Boulevard, Kissimmee; 407-847-4343
  Hours: Daily 9:00 a.m. to 3:15 p.m.
  Prices: Start at Adults $39, Children (under 5 and under 45 pounds) $17 for beginner trails
  Enjoy western-style riding on over 700 acres of beautiful wooded trails. Horse World offers beginner (nature trail), intermediate, and advanced trails, and lessons.

Fishing

- A #1 Bass Guide Service, P.O. Box 7544, Indian Lake Estate; 800-707-5463
- Big Toho Marina, 101 Lake Shore Boulevard, Kissimmee; 407-846-2124

Golf

- Celebration Golf Club, 701 Golf Park Drive, Celebration; 407-566-GOLF
- Champions Gate Golf Club, 1400 Masters Boulevard, Champions Gate; 407-787-4653
- Falcon's Fire Golf Club, 3200 Seralago Boulevard, Kissimmee; 407-397-2777
- Kissimmee Bay Country Club, 2801 Kissimmee Bay Boulevard, Kissimmee; 407-348-GOLF
- Mystic Dunes Golf Club, 900 Mystic Dunes, Kissimmee, 407-787-5678
- Remington Golf Club, 2995 Remington Boulevard, Kissimmee; 407-344-4004

Hotels Near the Ballpark

- Gaylord Palms, 6000 West Osceola Parkway, Kissimmee; 407-586-6338
- Holiday Inn Downtown, 2009 West Vine Street, Kissimmee; 407-846-2713
- Seralago Hotel and Suites — Main Gate East, 5678 West Irlo Bronson Memorial Highway (U.S. 192) Kissimmee; 407-396-4488
- Quality Inn Suites, 5876 West Irlo Bronson Memorial Highway (U.S. 192), Kissimmee; 407-396-8040
- Advantage Vacation Homes, 7799 Styles Boulevard, Kissimmee; 407-396-2262

They don't dodge autographs!

Second baseman Jeff Kent fields eager fans.

Photos courtesy of the Los Angeles Dodgers.

Pitcher Eric Gagne signs with a smile.

Chapter 10

Los Angeles Dodgers
Holman Stadium

At Dodgertown in Vero Beach

If you can make it to only one Spring Training site in Florida, this is the one you must visit. No other park in Florida captures the feeling of old-time Spring Training as well as Dodgertown's Holman Stadium in Vero Beach. It is the poster child for Spring Training as it ought to be.

Sure, it's difficult to find because it is hidden away from the main highways. And truth to tell, the seats are not that comfortable. There's really not a lot of shade, and the parking is scattered throughout the complex.

Once the game starts, however, you're transported back to a place and time where baseball is a game of youth. A place where you are reminded of the days when you and your friends found some sand lot, made bases out of boxes, and started whacking the ball as far as you could send it. No other Spring Training ballpark brings you as close to the players as this one. No other park lets you see as clearly what type of person each player is. And no other park welcomes autograph seekers as warmly. In short, it's fantastic.

Seeing the Los Angeles Dodgers in Vero Beach is an experience you'll want to give yourself plenty of time to enjoy. Get to the ballpark early. Holman Stadium is one of the few Grapefruit League parks that opens its practice fields to fans before the game. This gives you a wonderful opportunity to see players outside the glare of the game. For instance, at Spring Training 2003, I watched pitcher Kevin Brown rub it in to

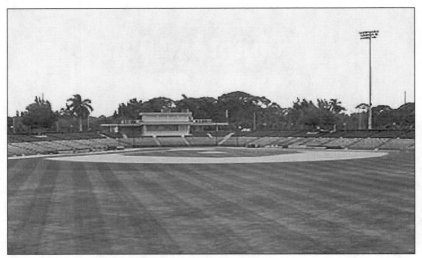

Photo courtesy of the Los Angeles Dodgers.

players in other positions after his ball repeatedly screamed over the fence. A pitcher's not supposed to be able to hit like that, but Brown did. Watching practice is also a great way to see the difference between the minor league players and the big leaguers. While the minor league players are running wind sprints and doing other exercises, the big leaguers are leisurely warming up. An added benefit of walking the practice fields is that you're sure to catch a couple of home-run or foul balls to keep as souvenirs.

One of the joys of this park is that every player is accessible to the fans on his way from the practice fields to the stadium. To get there, each has to walk (or ride a golf cart) over a bridge and through the parking lot, both of which are open to fans. You can stand on the bridge and walk through the lot with your favorite players. In fact, the players enter the stadium through the same entrance as the fans do.

Enter the stadium and you can tell that you're in a different world. You walk up a garden pathway to what is technically the main concourse and find that all the seats are below it. The stadium looks as if they simply pushed the dirt to the outside and put the ballpark in the middle. You'll also notice something very strange and different: there are no dugouts. There are just areas where the players sit behind a chain link fence.

Every seat in the stadium is close to the field and you can get very close to the players. They are literally within a foot or two of the stands while they wait for their turn at bat. (If you sit on the front row, you'll be able to spit your sunflower seeds onto the warning track.) You're also going to get a better view of the bullpen here than you will at any other ballpark. All of which makes watching a game here unlike watching one anywhere else.

You'll get a chance to meet some of the historical Dodger greats during your visit. The team brings its all-star broadcast line-up to Spring Training. If you sit near the press box, you can listen to Vin Scully and Rick Monday call the game while you watch it. Vin Scully, who has called Dodger games for 56 years, is a legend in baseball. It's worth the admission just to hear him live.

There are some drawbacks, of course. There is no shade for any of the stands, and if it rains, you will get wet. The seats are adequate, but a whole lot more comfortable if you bring your own cushion. Except for a tent at the front gate, the concession stands are concentrated in a single area in the center of the stadium, which gets packed, and the selection is limited. That's not to say there aren't options. On ground level of the third base side, for instance, you will find a rather large picnic area with a stand that offers grilled hamburgers and cheeseburgers. You can eat them sitting at a picnic table next to a duck pond — just like a day at the park except that the best of Spring Training is just a few yards away.

This is the way Spring Training was meant to be. It's the way it's been practiced for over 50 years in Vero Beach — without renovating the stadium and without limiting access to the players. Don't miss it. If you can visit only one Spring Training site, make it Dodgertown.

Fast Facts

Holman Stadium - Dodgertown
4101 26th Street
Vero Beach, FL 32960
772-569-6858
http://losangeles.dodgers.mlb.com

Getting There

Take I-95 to Exit 147, SR 60 East (Osceola Boulevard). Follow it to 43rd Avenue and take a left. Follow 43rd to 26th Street and take a right. The stadium is just ahead.

Parking

Is there a parking lot? It's more like there are lots of little parking lots spread throughout Dodgertown, some close to the stadium, others a bit of a walk. The walk from several of the parking lots is through the practice fields and will result in several stops and starts as you pause to watch the action on the field or wait for golf carts taxiing the players from their parking lot to the field to pass you. The key, as always, is getting here early. The earlier you get to the park, the shorter your walk.

Cost: $5

Tickets

Surprisingly, tickets are almost always available at Holman Stadium. Although the stadium is just average in size, I was able to get seats about two sections from the end of the stadium just one week before the game. I was then able to move to the front row on the other side of the stadium after I got there.

On average, about a third of tickets go unsold. Two factors probably account for this: Vero Beach is a small city, and it is further away from a major metropolitan area than any of the other Spring Training sites. It's a shame more people don't travel to this park.

There really are no bad seats in the stadium, and all seats are reserved and sell for the same price, $16 ($18 on weekends), whether you sit right behind home plate or at the very end of the outfield lines. That puts it among the lowest top ticket prices in the Grapefruit League and on a par with or a bit higher than most other parks' lower-priced reserved seats.

I used to lament the lack of a general admission ticket to the expansive berm in the outfield. No more. Holman now sells berm tickets for many games.

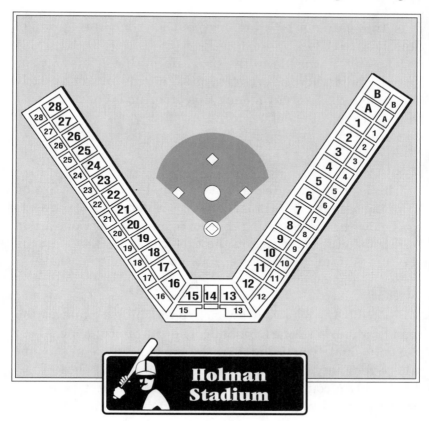

Capacity: 6,474
Average Attendance: 4,835
Ticket Prices:
   All seats reserved $16 weekdays, $18 nights/weekends
   Berm $8 (not available for all games)
For Tickets: 772-569-6858

Programs

Wow! What a program! It's thick. It has mug shots of every player. It has stats. It has a numerical roster. It has a complete biography plus career highlights for every player, manager, and trainer on the team. It's focused on Vero Beach and the surrounding area. In short, it has just about everything you could want in a program. For instance, there is a section on the top prospects in the Dodger organization. For non-Dodger fans, this may not be a big deal, but for their core group of fans, it sure is.

The only downside to the program is that it may be too heavily weighted to advertisements. There is an ad on nearly every page. Still, for my money, this program is one of the best in the Grapefruit League.

Cost: $4

Seats

This is probably the easiest place to find your seats in Spring Training because there is only one type of ticket. All of the seats are below the main seating concourse, and the sections are in numerical order starting on the first base side. Go up one of the ramps from the entrance, and you will find your seat.

Shade

Probably the biggest drawback to watching a game at Holman Stadium is the lack of shade. There is almost none. About the only shade you'll find is at the top of a couple of sections where four large trees cast their shadows. And those trees shade only a couple of rows. If you sit on the first base side, expect to have your face in the sun. On the third base side, you'll have your back and side to the sun. Wherever you sit, wear a lot of sunscreen.

Food & Drink

The Dodgertown people understand the need for consistency, and that includes offering the food that makes Dodger fans drool. You can order the staple of Los Angeles' fans, the Dodger Dog, here at Holman Stadium. While it isn't that thick, the Dodger Dog is a special hot dog that's extra tasty and snaps like a good hot dog. Otherwise, you'll find the usual ballpark eats.

To check out the offerings, go to the top center portion of the stadium. You'll find a series of concession stands, each offering different items. Or go to the grill on the ground floor on the third base side for a burger. The meat is taken right off the grill and put on your bun — a real treat. Still I'd stick with the Dodger Dog. When you have Dodger Dogs, is there anything else you really need?

Souvenirs

There's not a huge choice of souvenirs at Holman Stadium, but I did find some high-end Dodger memorabilia in addition to the traditional items. Perhaps my favorite was a clock in the shape of a Dodger pennant. I did not see anything like it at the other Spring Training parks.

If you want to shop, your best bet is to go to the small store outside the main entrance. As you face the gate, it's just to the right. The choice is limited and most of the items are behind the counter, but you'll find smaller crowds and shorter lines here than at the two small novelties stands inside the stadium. The inside stands are across the hall from the concessions. Again, all of the merchandise is behind the counter. The crowds here, however, make it tough to buy.

Dodgertown has tried to increase the souvenir offerings with a new addition. At the front gate, stadium officials have added a tent with ample and unique souvenirs. The tent is crowded and not very fan-friendly, but it's still better than the counter inside the stadium.

Tip: Looking for a way to get a souvenir for less than the normal price? Check out Holman's "Guess-your-pitch-speed machines." The stadium gives out batting helmets to winners. Just remember, your third pitch in a row is generally slower than your first two pitches.

Autographs

This is autograph city for those who can't wait to get their favorite player's signature. The easiest way to get an autograph is to get to the stadium early and wait outside. Across the parking lot from the main entrance is a bridge that connects the practice fields to the stadium. Every player, both Dodger and visitor, has to walk or ride a golf cart across that bridge to get to the stadium. Players are usually quite willing to sign if you are willing to walk with them.

That's not the only way to get an autograph here. You can get them near third base right before the game. After warm-ups, players are willing to sign as they walk to their bench. It's just a matter of asking them politely. Star shortstop Nomar

Garciaparra, for instance, repeats the same procedure before every game. He does his warm-ups, kneels for a five-minute prayer, and then walks over to sign autographs. Wait until after he is finished praying to ask.

Finally, as the game winds down, situate yourself as far down the first base line as you can get. Most players will walk down the first base wall and sign for you. I got nearly every player I wanted to sign a baseball.

In one of the stranger sights of my visit to Holman one year, all-star outfielder Shawn Green came out in a golf cart during a rain delay and signed autographs. It was just one more example of the wonderful spirit of Holman Stadium and the way the Dodgers appreciate their fans.

A Game or an Experience?

This park is literally a shrine to Spring Training. It's an historical treasure that can and should be experienced. The stadium and complex were designed by Dodger greats Walter O'Malley (manager) and Branch Rickey (front office), two of baseball's best ever people. The history alone would be enough to make your experience here more than just a game.

In the past, live music and picnic tables were just outside the park, but in 2006, this area became the new souvenir tent.

Up Close & Personal?

Perhaps the best feature of this stadium is how close it puts you to the players. In today's Spring Training, many parks discourage fan-player interaction. Here, they invite it. When the players are in their dugouts, they literally have their backs on the fence that is right in front of the fans seated behind the dugouts and behind the bullpens on either side of the stadium. You could reach out and touch them. (You'd probably be thrown out of the stadium if you did, but you could do it.) But even if you are as far from the field as possible, you won't have a bad seat. There are only about 30 rows of seats total, so even those at the very top are close to the action.

Tip: If you want a fun spot, take a seat down the first base line. You'll see every Dodger player up close as he walks back to the clubhouse.

Getting Away

It is surprisingly easy to get out of Holman Stadium. Thanks to the many small lots, there's no slowdown created by hundreds of cars trying to leave a single lot at the same time. There were only about 50 cars where we parked, meaning we weren't jostling for position or stuck in a bottleneck on our way out.

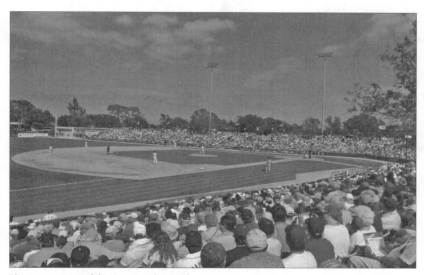

Photos courtesy of the Los Angeles Dodgers.

Spring training practically puts fans on the field with their heroes.

Before & After the Game: Restaurants

- Melody Inn, 1309 19th Place, Vero Beach; 772-770-2071
- Sonny's Real Pit Bar-B-Q, 5001 20th Street, Vero Beach; 772-770-4190
- Ocean Grill, Route 60 at the Ocean, Vero Beach; 772-231-5409
- R J Gators Hometown Grill and Bar, 6200 20th Street, Vero Beach; 772-562-1400
- Big Apple Pizza, 5970 20th Street, Vero Beach; 772-569-8900

Before & After the Game: Sports Bars

- Beef 'O'Brady's, 782 South U.S. Highway 1, Vero Beach; 772-794-2059
- Bobby's Restaurant and Lounge, 3450 Ocean Drive, Vero Beach; 772-231-6996

Before & After the Game: Attractions

Like many of the smaller Spring Training communities, Vero Beach does not have a lot of attractions outside of baseball and outdoor recreation. It is baseball, the beach, and little else. Still, there are a few other things to do. For more information, consult the Indian River County Chamber of Commerce web site, www.indianriverchamber.com, as well as the Florida state tourism web site, www.flausa.com.

- Vero Beach Train Station, 2336 14th Avenue, Vero Beach; 772-778-3435, www.irchistory.org
  Hours: Monday to Friday 10:00 a.m. to 4:00 p.m.
  Admission: Free
  Built in 1903, the station now houses the Indian River County Historical Society.
- Vero Beach Museum of Art, 3001 Riverside Park Drive, Vero Beach; 772-231-0707
  Hours: Monday to Saturday 10:00 a.m to 4:30 p.m., Sunday 1:00 to 4:30 p.m.
  Admission: General admission is free; donations accepted. Fees vary for special events and exhibits.

Offers art exhibitions and a sculpture garden.
- Indian River Citrus Museum / Heritage Center, 2140 14th Avenue, Vero Beach; 772-770-2263
Hours: Tuesday to Friday 10:00 a.m. to 4:00 p.m.
Admission: Free.
The artifacts, photographs, and memorabilia of the Indian River County citrus pioneers can be found here.
- The Sebastian Fishing Museum, Sebastian Inlet State Recreation Area, 9700 South A1A, Melbourne Beach; 772-388-2750
Hours: Daily 10:00 a.m. to 4:00 p.m.
Admission: Museum free, state park fees apply (772-589-9659 for park information)
Located on the south side of Sebastian Inlet State Park, the museum focuses on the history of Sebastian's fishing industry and its pioneers.
- Environmental Learning Center, 255 Live Oak Drive, Wabasso Causeway, Vero Beach; 772-589-5050, www.elcweb.org
Hours: Tuesday to Friday 10:00 a.m. to 4:00 p.m., Saturday 9:00 a.m. to noon, Sunday 1:00 p.m. to 4:00 p.m.
Admission: Free
This nature center on Wabasso Island offers a hands-on approach to investigating the environment. You can walk through a mangrove forest, a butterfly garden, wet labs, and more. It offers one-hour tours on weekends.

Before & After the Game: Activities

Surf, kayak, canoe, hike, fish, play golf, and more. Here are some listings to get you started:
- Vero's Tackle and Sport Shop, 57 Royal Palm Pointe, Vero Beach; 772-567-6550
- Indian River Kayak & Canoe, 3435 Aviation Boulevard, Vero Beach; 772-569-5757

Golf

- Orchid Island Golf & Beach Club, One Beachside Drive, Orchid; 772-388-2350

- Quail Valley Golf Club, 6545 Pinnacle Drive, Vero Beach; 772-299-0093
- The Windsor Club, 3125 Windsor Boulevard, Vero Beach; 772-388-5050
- Sebastian Municipal Golf Club, Main Street, Sebastian; 772-589-6801

Hotels Near the Ballpark

- Best Western, 8797 20th Street, Vero Beach; 772-567-8321
- Budget Inn, 2022 U.S. Highway 1, Vero Beach; 772-567-4331
- Citrus Motel, 3256 North U.S. Highway 1, Vero Beach; 772-562-4163
- Hampton Inn, 9350 19th Lane, Vero Beach; 772-770-4299
- Holiday Inn Express, 9400 19th Lane, Vero Beach; 772-567-2500
- Howard Johnson's Downtown, 1725 U.S. Highway 1, Vero Beach; 772-567-5171
- Vero Motel, 3116 U.S. Highway 1, Vero Beach; 772-564-2142
- Howard Johnson Express Inn, 1985 90th Avenue, Vero Beach; 772-778-1985
- Disney's Vero Beach Resort, 9250 Island Grove Terrace, Vero Beach; 772-234-2000

Chapter 11

Minnesota Twins
Bill Hammond Stadium

Fort Myers

As we go to press, there is word that Hammond Stadium is scheduled to undergo renovations and construction, to be completed by the beginning of Spring Training 2007. Several details are still unconfirmed, but a July 2006 story in the Naples Daily News *informs us that there will be a new berm for lawn seating and standing room, to be installed along right field, where the visitors' bullpen was previously located, as well as a new concession area by the new berm, and a couple of rows of premium seating behind home plate. While these changes will render some of this chapter obsolete, we look forward to being pleasantly surprised in the coming season!*

From outside, Bill Hammond Stadium is one of the more picturesque sites in the Grapefruit League. A row of palm trees lines the approach. A beautiful water fountain and sculpture grace the center front, and the stadium blends in with the region's architecture, right down to its tin roof and abundance of windows.

It's unfortunate that the beauty does not continue inside the stadium. Inside, Bill Hammond Stadium is just a stadium. It's big, metallic, and filled with cement. It lacks the charm of its neighbor, City of Palms Park, where the Red Sox play, and tries too much to imitate a Major League ballpark. There are few places here where you can get autographs.

Bill Hammond Stadium is just plain white inside with no bright colors to catch the eye. The grandstands are too high,

Photo by Al Larson, courtesy of the Minnesota Twins.

putting the seats at the top quite a distance from the field, and they end just a few sections away from the dugouts instead of extending out to flank the outfield. The small roof covers relatively few seats, and there is only one spot to buy souvenirs, though that's likely to change with the new construction.

That said, there are plenty of pleasant surprises in this park. For instance, the food is some of the best in the Grapefruit League. There are lots of options in addition to the traditional baseball fare of hot dogs, peanuts, and Cracker Jacks, including healthy meal options (which may strike some fans as downright subversive). There is a little sit-down bar hidden at the end of the main concourse on the third base side where you can get almost any kind of beer you would want, imported or domestic. To catch a glimpse of your favorite stars, you can go up to the second level of the stadium on the third base side and watch the practice field, the bullpen, and other sites. It's a nice view.

Still, the stadium as a whole fails to capture the essence of Spring Training. If you want that, you need to spend the extra money and go to City of Palms Park in downtown Fort Myers. At Bill Hammond Stadium, you're teased with beauty outside only to find an average stadium within, though we're hoping the proposed changes will make the ballpark experience here lots more fun for fans.

Fast Facts

Hammond Stadium at Lee County Sports Complex
14100 Six Mile Cypress Parkway
Fort Myers, FL 33912
800-33-TWINS
http://minnesota.twins.mlb.com

Getting There

Take Interstate 75 to Exit 131, Daniels Parkway/Airport. Go west for two miles to Six Mile Cypress Parkway. Turn left and the stadium will be on your right.

Parking

It's wonderful how close the parking lot is to the stadium. Few ballparks boast closer parking. And the walk from your car is downright picturesque. You walk along a grassy stretch lined with palm trees, all the while looking at the gorgeous stadium in the distance. As at most parks, the later you arrive, the longer your walk because the parking for Bill Hammond Stadium does not wrap around the ballpark. It is one long lot. You park on grass but the drives are paved.

Cost: $5

Tickets

This is a difficult ticket to get, perhaps because all the people who can't get tickets to see the Red Sox at nearby City of Palms Park travel here. On average, there are fewer than 400 tickets available on game day. Also, do not make the mistake of thinking that it will be easier to get a ticket to a Twins vs. Red Sox game here than it would be at City of Palms Park. It isn't. I made that mistake and I was lucky to get a standing room only ticket here. The Red Sox are just as big a draw at Bill Hammond Stadium as they are at any other stadium in the Grapefruit League. So buy your tickets early if you are planning on seeing the Red Sox or any of the other marquee teams play here.

Ticket prices are about average for the Grapefruit League.

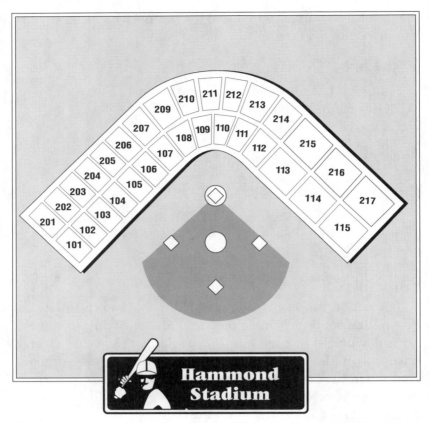

Note: There are several seating additions planned for Spring Training '07, but new seating charts are not yet available as we go to press. We include this chart for reference purposes.

But there has been no general admission in the past, so there were no cheap seats. This is likely to change with the opening of berm seating.

Note: Hammond Stadium is unusual in that the upper (200 number) sections are bleacher seats. Be forewarned: they're metal with no armrests. If that doesn't bother you, they're fine. If you want comfort, aim for a seat in the 100 sections.

Capacity: 7,500
Average Attendance: 7,151
Ticket Prices:
    Box Seats $20
    Reserved $18
For Tickets: 800-33-TWINS

Programs

The program here is probably the best investment of any in the Grapefruit League. It has just about anything you could want. There are plenty of statistics for the die-hard baseball fan, yet enough interesting articles about the team and the area to keep non-fans happy. There are mug shots of every player. There are instructions on how to keep score (some of the best you'll find anywhere, although they are not on the page with the scorecard). For Twins fans, there is plenty of copy about the farm teams and their promising minor league players, along with Twins trivia and a crossword puzzle that is mostly devoted to Twins trivia. In addition, there is a list of advertisers. If you are looking for restaurants or other attractions in the area, that comes in handy because you can scan the list of ads and find a restaurant or an activity you may want to try.

What I liked best about the program were the articles about the area's Spring Training history. There were sections devoted to Spring Training records, both team and individual, as well as a great article on Fort Myers' long history with baseball.

The program does have a few flaws. There is no numerical listing of the 40-man roster, only an alphabetical one, and the player profiles are scattered throughout the book. That makes individual profiles a bit harder to find than they would be if they were all in one place. In addition, while there is a list of upcoming promotions at the stadium — and written directions to find restrooms, concessions, and novelties — there is no stadium diagram to be found. But those are small flaws considering all the things this program does right and its modest price.

Cost: $3

Seats

Finding your seat is a breeze here. There are plenty of entrances and exits, and great signage. If you have a reserved seat, you enter the stadium's main seating aisle and go up when you get to your section. If you have a box or premium seat, you go down. Keep an eye out for signage directing you to the new berm.

Shade

It is essential to wear sunscreen here. The very small roof covers only the top of the stadium. Sit anywhere else and you are in the sun for most of the game. You will get some relief on the third base side once the sun goes behind the stadium, which is fairly early because of the stadium's height.

Food & Drink

The concessions may be the best thing about Bill Hammond Stadium. There are plenty of options, from turkey legs to frozen lemonade. The jumbo hot dog is just that, very jumbo. In fact, the hot dog is too big for the bun. I would stick with something else, like the turkey leg.

Beer drinkers will love this stadium. It may have the best selection of beer anywhere in the Grapefruit League — but only at the bar. The regular concession stands serve the usual Budweiser and Bud Light. For the good stuff, go to the end of the stadium on the third base side. There you will find hidden a little bar that serves all sorts of bottled beer and a selection of imports on tap. The bar area has shaded picnic tables and a television. It's crowded during most of the game. By the time you visit, an additional concession area may be open near the new berm along right field.

Souvenirs

While Bill Hammond Stadium has a wonderful selection of food and drink, its novelties selection is limited. There is nothing novel here, just the traditional baseball items. All the merchandise is in a single store on the main concourse.

Autographs

Don't count on getting autographs here. Because of the layout — players enter and exit the through the dugouts — there are few opportunities to ask Twins for their signatures.

Your best bet is either to arrive or leave early. Then stake your claim to a place in the aisle in front of the first row of seats on the side of the Twins dugout closer to home plate. Occasionally a player will come over to sign. Even more occasionally, players will sign on the side of the dugout closer to the outfield, and sometimes, but not often, players will stop and sign in front of the dugout. In this case, you have to toss your autographable item over the dugout to the player. Make sure you have the player's attention before tossing anything.

On the visitors' side, there was a small area of empty space near the field, at the end of the stands next to the first row of seats. All the visiting players had to walk by this spot to get to the field. I'm hoping the addition of berm seating will improve fans' odds of getting autographs on this side of the field.

I also spotted a roped-off area outside the ballpark on the northwest side of the stadium. Players have to walk along it to get from the practice fields to the stadium. While I didn't see autographing activity there, it may be just a matter of timing.

A Game, or an Experience?

The minor league team that plays in Bill Hammond Stadium during the summer season is tied to Bill Veeck, the 1970s innovator who created many of the promotions and fan contests that have become staples in today's baseball. So it's no surprise that the stadium's operators go heavy on them. Nearly every Spring Training game offers a special promotion of some kind and nearly every inning features some sort of fan contest, with the contestants randomly picked through a drawing of seat numbers. I went on t-shirt day and got a free t-shirt. The most entertaining contest I saw was one in which two fans were dressed up in sumo wrestler outfits and had it out on the field.

Up Close & Personal?

The first few rows here are pretty close to the action, and the planned premium seats behind home plate should add to that number. During batting practice, you can overhear the conversations and clearly see the interactions between the players. If you sit anywhere else in this rather large stadium, it's difficult to get close to the players. At the top, you'll feel like you're at a Major League game.

The location of the bullpens also cuts your access to the players. They are situated beyond the ends of the stands. You can't see the pitchers warm up unless you sit in the very last seats, at the end of the first or third base line. Even then, you'll be watching from a distance. This may change for the better — at least on the visitors' side — if the visitors' bullpen is moved as planned, to make way for lawn seating.

Getting Away

There is only one way out of the parking lot, but you won't wait long. The stadium empties onto a four-lane road and the police are quick to stop traffic to let people out. So it's just a matter of waiting your turn to get out of the lot itself.

Before & After the Game: Restaurants

The following restaurants are all located in Fort Myers.
- The Prawnbroker, 13451 McGregor Boulevard; 239-489-2226
- Big Olaf Creamery, 117 Bell Tower Shops, Daniels Parkway and U.S. Highway 41; 239-590-9195
- Bistro 41, 143 Bell Tower Shops, Daniels Parkway and U.S. Highway 41; 239-466-4141
- D'Amico & Sons, 201 Bell Tower Shops, Daniels Parkway and U.S. Highway 41; 239-489-0001
- Johnny Rockets, 221 Bell Tower Shops, Daniels Parkway and U.S. Highway 41; 239-415-1920
- Romano's Macaroni Grill, 13721 South Tamiami Trail; 239-433-7786
- The Ale House, 4400 Kernel Circle; 239-931-4160

Before & After the Game: Sports Bars

The following sports bars are all located in Fort Myers.
- Potts Sports Cafe, 6900 Daniels Parkway; 239-768-5500
- Shoeless Joe's, 13051 Bell Tower Drive (in the lobby of the Holiday Inn Select); 239-437-0650
- Stevie Tomato's Sports Page, 11491 South Cleveland Avenue; 239-939-7211

Before & After the Game: Attractions:

Fort Myers is home to two Spring Training stadiums. So many of the offerings below will also be found in Chapter 4. I repeat them here so that you don't have to flip back and forth in the book. The county's official website for tourism is www.leeislandcoast.com.

- The Big M Casino, 450 Harbor Court, Fort Myers Beach; 888-373-3521, 239-765-PLAY, www.bigmcasino.com
  Hours: Sails Tuesday to Sunday, 10:15 a.m. and 6:00 p.m.
  Cost: Morning cruise $10. Evening cruise $10 except Friday and Saturday $20.
  This luxurious gaming yacht offers Las Vegas-style casino gambling on its two daily sailings from Moss Marine on Fort Myers Beach. Cruises last five and a half (evening cruise) to six hours (morning). A buffet and a la carte dining are extra. You must be 21 to sail. Reservations are required.

- Edison-Ford Winter Estates, 2350 McGregor Boulevard, Fort Myers; 888-377-9475, 239-334-7419, www.edison-ford-estate.com
  Hours: Daily 9:00 a.m. to 5:30 p.m., last tour at 4:00 p.m
  Admission: Adults $20, Children (6 to 12) $11. (Cheaper options limiting visits to certain areas are also available.)
  Tour the winter homes of Thomas Edison and his neighbor and friend Henry Ford. Tours include Edison's botanical gardens, lab, and museum, as well as both homes.

- Imaginarium Hands-On Museum, 2000 Cranford Avenue, Fort Myers; 239-337-3332
  Hours: Monday to Saturday 10:00 a.m. to 5:00 p.m., Sunday noon to 5:00 p.m.
  Admission: Adults $8, Seniors (55+) $7, Children (3 to 12) $5
  Features hands-on exhibits, including a hurricane simulator and fossil dig, along with aquatic exhibits such as a 550-gallon coral reef tank, a 190-gallon fresh water lagoon, and a touch tank. "Hands-On Fun Shows" at 11:00 a.m. and 2:00 p.m.

- Mike Greenwell's Family Fun Park, 35 Pine Island Road, Cape Coral; 239-574-4386
  Hours: Sunday to Thursday 10:00 a.m. to 10:00 p.m., Friday and Saturday 10:00 a.m. to 11:00 p.m.
  Admission: Free; cost of rides and activities varies

Former Red Sox outfielder Mike Greenwell owns this amusement center. It offers a fish feeding dock, a paintball arena, bumper cars, a playground, miniature golf, batting cages, four go-cart tracks, a snack bar, and a 6,000-square-foot arcade.

Before & After the Game: Activities

Fishing

- Back Country Fishing Charters with Captain Paul Hobby, 13371 Electron Drive, Fort Myers; 239-433-1007
- One More Cast Charters, 14869 Kimberly Lane, Fort Myers; 239-454-4934
- Captain Tony's Fishing Adventures, 18800 San Carlos Boulevard, Fort Myers Beach; 239-415-0515
- Joyce Rehr's Fly Fishing & Light Tackle Guide Service, 1155 Buttonwood Lane, Sanibel; 239-472-3308

Golf

- Gateway Golf & Country Club, 11360 Championship Drive, Fort Myers; 239-561-1010
- Shell Point Golf Club, 16401 On Par Boulevard, Fort Myers; 239-433-9790
- Beachview Golf Course, 1100 Parview Drive, Sanibel; 239-472-2626
- Gulf Harbour Yacht & Country Club, 14490 Vista River Drive, Fort Myers; 239-437-0881

Hotels Near the Ballpark

The following hotels are all located in Fort Myers.
- Best Western Airport Inn, 8955 Daniels Parkway; 239-561-7000
- Comfort Suites - Airport, 13651 Indian Paint Lane; 239-768-0005
- Holiday Inn Select Fort Myers - Airport, 13051 Bell Tower Drive; 877-617-4768 (toll free), 239-482-2900
- Wynstar Inn & Suites, 10150 Daniels Parkway; 239-791-5000, 866-791-5000 (toll free)
- Sleep Inn - Airport, 13661 Indian Paint Lane; 239-561-1117

Chapter 12

New York Mets
Tradition Field

Port St. Lucie

Can $10 million make a stadium perfect? No, but that amount of money certainly went a long way to improving Tradition Field, the spring home of the New York Mets. The improvements made after the 2003 Spring Training season have moved the stadium up the charts from one of the worst in the Grapefruit League to above average. The one major flaw that remains could only be remedied by replacing the stadium with a new one.

That flaw is the stadium's size. While capacity is about average, the park looks big, especially from inside the stadium. That's because most of the seats are packed into relatively small grandstands. Instead of stretching the stands out to the end of the first and third base lines, the stands end just a few sections past the dugouts. As a result, many seats are high above the playing field. But the renovation did add a few rows of additional seating right behind home plate. If you sit in there, you'll be really close to the action.

It also seems easier to get autographs now. Before the improvements, you were relegated to asking for autographs on the Mets practice fields two hours before the game. Now, you can get an autograph or two right from the field, because the bullpen has been moved close to the new seating area.

The ballpark also looks better, inside and out. As you walk up to the stadium, you'll immediately spot new signage, a brick façade, and better fencing. Together, they give Tradition Field

Photo courtesy of the New York Mets.

the look of the old time stadiums.

Inside, the most impressive change is the addition of a berm just past the right field wall. While other stadiums have berms that are bigger or taller, this one has restrooms and a concession stand at the top. The roof is a special plus if there is a quick rainstorm or you find you need to get out of the sun.

Another nifty addition is terrace level seating, complete with picnic tables on tiers where you can sit and watch the game. You have to buy a special ticket to sit at the tables, but you can walk through them from the grandstands to get autographs.

Be warned, however, you can't get from the grandstands to the berm and bleachers if the game is sold out. Those areas require a separate ticket and are reached through a separate entrance.

New concession stands round out the improvements. They serve a variety of tasty food, including a knish.

As in the past, Tradition Field is still the most entertaining ballpark in the Grapefruit League, outside of Disney's stadium. There is a contest before almost every inning and they blast music every time a Met comes to bat. The stadium also offers a great balance of sun and shade.

When you go to Tradition Field, expect to feel like you are in Queens or Brooklyn. Almost everyone at the stadium speaks with a thick New York accent. They are fanatical about their team and their hatred for the Yankees. Do not show up in pin stripes; you will probably get beat up.

Of course, love or hate New York teams, you have to respect their fans. They are some of the most knowledgeable anywhere. They can tell you about every prospect, every statistic, and why their team either will be very bad or will win the World Series this year. There is no in between.

Fast Facts

Tradition Field
525 Northwest Peacock Boulevard
Port St. Lucie, FL 34986
772-871-2115
http://newyork.mets.mlb.com
http://www.traditionfield.com

Getting There

Take I-95 to Exit 121, St. Lucie West Boulevard East. Go about half a mile east and turn left onto Northwest Peacock Boulevard. The stadium is straight ahead about 2.5 miles.

Parking

The parking lot is fairly close to the stadium. It's across a small street and it actually wraps around the front of the stadium. So you won't have to walk too far regardless of when you get to the stadium. While the lot is unpaved, you won't find many of the hazards of other grassy parking lots, such as anthills.

A neat thing about parking here is that the players' lot is close by, behind a chain link fence. It is not uncommon to see Mets players with their families as they get into their cars and drive away.

Tip: Parking on the western side of the lot will put you close to the entrance to the practice fields.

Cost: $5

Tickets

It is surprising how many tickets are available to purchase on the day of the game. On average, there are more than 2,000 tickets left on game day. Perhaps it is because of their location 40 miles from the next major metro area, West Palm Beach. While its top seat is among the highest priced in the League, the stadium's general admission ticket price ties with Bradenton's as the lowest (excepting only Fort Lauderdale's kid-priced general admission).

Capacity: 7,347

Average Attendance: 5,191

Ticket Prices:

Premium Box $25

Field Level Terrace $20

Lower Box $15

Upper Reserved $10

Bleachers and Berm $6

For Tickets: 772-871-2115

Programs

The Mets field a large but mediocre program. It's printed on heavy, white non-glossy paper, so the pictures aren't as sharp as in many other programs. And there's not much to read — only three articles in the program I got. On the plus side, the Mets' program includes mug shots of every player, *Baseball America*'s feature on the team's upcoming prospects, a scorecard and instructions on how to keep score, and a numerical roster. However, the roster is mixed in with the rosters of every team the Mets play, and there is only one year of statistics on each of the players — even the stars. It would be nice to have more to read. Perhaps a recap of the previous season or an outlook for the future would provide better value for the consumer.

Cost: $5

Seats

It shouldn't be too hard to find your seats. There is an upper section, a lower section, bleachers, and a berm. You can tell where they are and where each section is. But that doesn't mean you won't have problems getting to your seat. If you are seated at the top of the stadium, as I was, the access to your row may be blocked by a camera stand. The stands are four to five feet square. They cross rows and cover several seats. Many people,

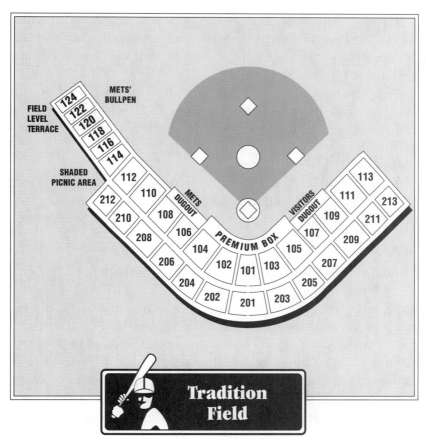

including me, climbed to the top of one section only to realize we could not access our seats without going back down.

To get to the berm or bleachers, you need to go to a separate entrance. If you are facing the ticket window, the entrance is around the stadium to the right. When the game is sold out, you must have a ticket for the berm or bleachers to get into this area. At other games, your grandstand ticket will get you in.

Shade

This is probably the best feature of this stadium. There is the perfect balance of shade and sun; everyone can be happy. If you are looking to sit in the shade, buy your tickets early and aim for the middle. The stadium is designed with a rather large roof that hangs over the center section. The sun is behind the roof for much of the game because the stadium faces north.

However, the sun shines on a significant percentage of seats. Any of the reserved seats near the end, especially those on the first base side, will get a lot of sun, as will all bleacher seats and (most likely) the berm.

Note: No seats are perfect for getting a suntan. Fans on the first base side have their back to the sun for most of the game and those on the third base side have their sides to the sun.

Food & Drink

Expect good food here with lots of options, including a knish and New York-style Italian ices. The ice I had was absolutely fantastic — refreshing, flavorful, and good to the last melted drop.

Souvenirs

One of the pluses of the renovations is better souvenir shopping. While the stock is limited to the usual items (t-shirts, balls, hats, and so on), the new store is much larger than its predecessor and the prices are clearly marked (a shortcoming in most ballparks). The store opens around 9:00 a.m., allowing you to buy a baseball or program in time to have it autographed during the team's morning practice. If you want to browse later without walking all the way back to the store, you'll find a couple of souvenir stands inside the park.

Autographs

Your best bet for getting an autograph is to get to the stadium about four hours before the game. You will be allowed into certain sections of the practice field and some of the Mets players will sign, not many, however. The team roster is filled with players who sign few autographs and refuse to acknowledge the fan's presence. However, some do sign. The key is to be able to walk with the players as they move from one practice field to the other.

You can also try for autographs during the game. Stand near the bullpen in the terrace field section or along the front row past the first base dugout. While it is still going to be tough to get a star's autograph, many of the players will come over and sign in these areas.

After the game, you'll have a chance at some players as

Photos courtesy of the New York Mets.

Fans enjoy a New York Mets night game at Traditions Field. Below, two views of the berm, which offers restrooms, concessions, and a roof for quick escapes from sudden rainstorms and too much March sun.

well. The players' parking lot is on the first base side of the stadium. Sometimes, players will come over on their way out and sign a few. It's hit and miss here, however.

A Game or an Experience?

With the exception of Cracker Jack Stadium at Walt Disney World's Wide World of Sports Complex, this is probably the most entertaining park in the Grapefruit League. Every time a Met comes to bat, they blast music. There is a contest before nearly every inning. They even go so far as to shoot t-shirts into the stands for fans to catch. They also have lots of special days with giveaways. The day I was there, it was bobble heads. Now many places give away bobble heads to, say, the first thousand fans. Here they gave everyone a ticket with one of four Mets stars' names on it. They then pulled one of the tickets and every fan with that player's name got a bobble head. That meant any family or group of four or more was guaranteed to get at least one free bobble head.

Up Close & Personal?

Tradition Field is an average-size Spring Training ballpark that looks much bigger than it is. In many respects it seems like a miniature Major League stadium. However, the improvements have created a number of opportunities for fans to get close to the players. Sitting in the new berm lets you connect with players before the game during warm-ups. The new seats behind home plate bring you close to the action throughout the game, and the terrace section puts you right next to the pitchers and catchers as they get ready to enter the game. So while the stadium is still big, seating most people far from the action, there are opportunities to savor the essence of the Spring Training experience.

Getting Away

A great system of roads leads out of the ballpark and quickly turn into a four-lane highway. From there, it's only a hop, skip, and jump to the Interstate. So even though there are only a couple of exits from the parking lot, you'll get away fast once you're out of the lot. And that's not likely to take long. The stadium averages about 70 percent capacity, so the lot empties fairly fast.

Before & After the Game: Restaurants

- Ankai Japanese Restaurant, 1353 Northwest St. Lucie West Boulevard, Port St. Lucie; 772-344-0464
- Bob Evans Restaurant, 1830 Southwest Fountainview Boulevard, Port St. Lucie; 772-879-0973
- Chili's Grill & Bar, 2050 Northwest Courtyard Circle, Port St. Lucie; 772-344-0021
- Little Italy, 1329 Northwest St. Lucie West Boulevard, Port St. Lucie; 772-878-4040
- McAlister's Deli, 220 Northwest Peacock Boulevard, Port St. Lucie; 772-871-1978
- Outback Steakhouse, 1950 Northwest Courtyard Circle, Port St. Lucie; 772-873-9990
- Palm City Grill, 1347 Northwest St. Lucie West Boulevard, Port St. Lucie; 772-343-8180
- Ruby Tuesday, 1500 Northwest Courtyard Circle, Port St. Lucie; 772-340-2575
- Zen Zen Chinese Restaurant, 896 Southwest St. Lucie West Boulevard, Port St. Lucie; 772-878-8000

Before & After the Game: Sports Bars

- Duffy's of Port St. Lucie, 790 Southwest St. Lucie West Boulevard, Port St. Lucie; 772-873-8150

Before & After the Game: Attractions

For other things to do before and after the game, see St. Lucie County's web site, www.visitstluciefla.com.

- Rave Motion Picture, 1900 Courtyard Circle, Port St. Lucie; 772-344-3570
  Hours and prices vary
  A 14-screen multiplex.
- SuperPlay USA, 1600 Northwest Courtyard Circle, Port St. Lucie; 772-408-5800, www.superplayusa.com
  Hours: Sunday to Thursday 9:00 a.m. to 11:00 p.m., Friday and Saturday 9:00 a.m. to 1:00 a.m.
  Cost: Varies

This entertainment center features duckpin bowling, miniature golf, batting cages, laser tag, and an arcade.

- Skatetown USA, 4301 Orange Avenue, Fort Pierce; 772-461-0266, www.skatetownflorida.com
  Hours: Wednesday 6:30 p.m. to 9:00 p.m., Friday 7:00 p.m. to 11:00 p.m., Saturday 10:00 a.m. to 4:00 p.m. and 7:30 p.m. to 11:00 p.m., Sunday 1:00 p.m. to 4:00 p.m.
  Cost: Varies

An indoor rink for inline skating; rentals available.

Before & After the Game: Activities

- Oxbow Eco-Center, 5400 Northeast St. James Drive, Port St. Lucie; 34983 772-785-5833
- Harbor Branch Oceanographic Institution, 5600 U.S. Highway 1 North, Ft. Pierce; 772-465-2400
- Manatee Observation and Education Center, 480 North Indian River Drive, Ft. Pierce; 772-466-1600
- The Savannas Recreational Area, 1400 East Midway Road, Ft. Pierce; 800-789-5776, 772-464-7855

Golf

- PGA Village, 9700 Reserve Boulevard, Port St. Lucie; 772-467-1299

Hotels Near the Ballpark

- Hampton Inn & Suites, 155 Southwest Peacock Boulevard, Port St. Lucie; 772-878-5900
- Holiday Inn – Port St. Lucie, 10120 South Federal Highway 1, Port St. Lucie; 772-337-2200
- Mainstay Suites, 8501 Champions Way, Port St. Lucie; 772-460-8882
- Sheraton's PGA Vacation Resort, 8702 Champions Way, Port St. Lucie; 772-460-5700
- Springhill Suites by Marriott, 2000 Northwest Courtyard Circle, Port St. Lucie; 772-871-2929
- Club Med's Sandpiper, 3500 Southeast Morningside Boulevard, Port St. Lucie; 772-398-5100

Chapter 13

New York Yankees
Legends Field

Tampa

"You've got to see Legends Field." That's what so many people say. Over and over again, whenever you talk to someone from the Tampa area, they brag about how great Legends Field is.

Don't believe the hype. Yes, Legends Field is a beautiful park. Its sculptured gardens, white façade, and the giant Yankees sign along the wall all make Legends Field a sight to behold. You can see it easily as you drive down Dale Mabry Highway to the stadium. But all of that cannot take away the fact that this stadium is more like a Major League ballpark than any other stadium in the Grapefruit League.

Quite simply, Legends Field is not a Spring Training stadium in any sense of the term. Start with the size of the ballpark. At over 10,000 seats, it is considerably larger than any other stadium in the Grapefruit League and almost a third the size of many Major League ballparks. (The field of play is exactly the same dimensions as Yankee Stadium in the Bronx.) The size creates an atmosphere that is anything but intimate. It creates a separation between fans and players that is made even worse by the stadium's policies and practices.

For instance, Legends Field is the only stadium where they will not let anyone but ticket holders with lower-level seats into the lower level section. When I was there, I lucked into some very good seats. They were behind home plate and I was looking straight down the first base line. I wanted to go

Photo by Kelly Monaghan.

to the field near the first base dugout, about 10 to 15 sections away from my seats, which were near the third base dugout. Thanks to stadium policy, I couldn't just walk down the aisle from the concourse. I had to walk back to my section, go down the aisle to the front, and then walk through the rows of seats back to the first base dugout.

It doesn't help that policemen stand guard at each end of the Yankees dugout throughout the game (to prevent any harassment of the players). It's a sight you don't associate with Spring Training, and it sure doesn't enhance the experience.

Also atypical of Spring Training is the lack of a solid corps of regular baseball fans. Much of the lower level is sold to corporate season-ticket holders who bought seats when the Yankees first started playing at Legends Field and the games were mostly at night. Now, the games are mostly during the day and many corporate ticket holders either cannot or do not come. That means lots of empty seats at sold-out games. And most games here do sell out. The New York Yankees have such a following that any place they play is hallowed ground, including Legends Field, despite its many drawbacks.

As for Yankee autographs, as a good New Yorker would say, Fuhgeddaboudit! You may get a few by the practice field if you're really lucky.

That's not to say that everything about Legends Field is bad. The stadium has the best concessions anywhere in the Grapefruit League, complete with an outpost of Outback Steakhouse. The souvenir program is great, and there is entertainment before the game.

The Yankees put on a spectacular opening day show. One recent opener featured a big marching band, a military special ops squad parachuting onto the field and about 60 GIs unfurling a huge American flag while the national anthem was sung by a pair of local celebrities, all capped off by fireworks. That day was also a great opportunity to see Yankees legends like Reggie Jackson and Yogi Berra in person.

Outside the ballpark, you'll also find a square devoted to all the great players the Yankees have had on their team over the years. They've dedicated a plaque to each one, complete with the player's name, number, and a brief biography.

One of the more interesting things about Legends Field is the number of Japanese fans you will see at the games. Since the Yankees signed Hideki Matsui, fans from his native Japan have been traveling to Tampa for Spring Training.

After finally experiencing what everyone said was such a great ballpark, I was glad to leave. Hopefully, this is not the future of Spring Training, but the exception.

If you are a Yankees fan, order your tickets early and make the trek. But make sure you also see the Yankees play at one of the other stadiums in the Tampa area so that you get to experience the real feel of Spring Training. And if you're not a Yankees fan, don't worry if you can't get tickets to a game at Legends Field. You'll get a more authentic Spring Training experience elsewhere.

Fast Facts

Legends Field
3802 Dr. Martin Luther King, Jr. Boulevard
Tampa, FL 33607
813-879-2244
http://newyork.yankees.mlb.com
http://www.legendsfieldtampa.com

Getting There

From I-275 West in Tampa, take Exit 41C, turn right at the bottom of the ramp onto Himes Street. Legends Field is about 1.7 miles north on your left. Turn left at Martin Luther King Jr. Boulevard; the parking lots will be on your left.

Parking

It's amazing what they make Yankees fans go through. I guess they feel if they have to ride a train to see them at home, they can walk a mile to get to the ballpark.

Parking here is on the other side of Dale Mabry Highway from the stadium. You have to park your car and walk to a bridge that crosses six-lane Dale Mabry. For this you pay one of the highest parking prices in the Grapefruit League.

Note: The lot you see just a few feet from the stadium's front gate is exclusively for corporate ticket holders. It's not only close, for them, it's free.

Cost: $7

Tickets

Buy your ticket as early as possible. This is one of the hardest tickets to get in the Grapefruit League. On average, there are only 65 tickets left on game day. This is not because of the Yankees' large fan base; it's because of the success the team has had in selling corporate season tickets. Most of the lower bowl seats are held by companies, and they are often empty.

If you didn't buy ahead and your heart is set on going to a Yankees game at Legends Field, you can try for a ticket to a game with one of the less popular teams. For instance, I got my ticket to a Yankees vs. Toronto Blue Jays game at the Legends Field's ticket window the morning of the game.

Note: There was some scalping outside the stadium, but surprisingly, not a lot. Be careful if you decide to go this route. Make sure you check your tickets carefully before handing off any money.

Although they're in great demand, Legends Field tickets are only slightly more expensive than the Grapefruit League average. Some stadiums that host lesser teams charge more.

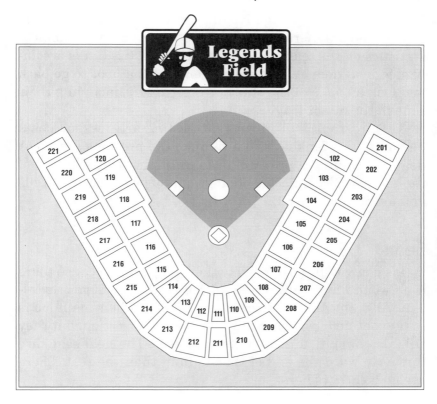

Capacity: 10,200
Average Attendance: 10,134
Ticket Prices:
    Lower Reserved $18
    Field Reserved $16
    Upper Reserved $15
    Upper Field Reserved $12
For Tickets: 813-879-2244

Programs

The program at Legends Field is perfect for a baseball fan. It has just about everything you could ask for. The only thing lacking is an easy way to identify the Yankees players, who do not have names on their uniforms. So you have to identify players by their numbers. The "Spring Training Roster" insert gives you uniform numbers, but it is arranged alphabetically by player, not numerically, which makes things a little harder.

But, that is the only negative in an otherwise great program. This is the only Grapefruit League program with complete statistics on the team's players. Each statistics box is accompanied by a mug shot of the player. It was a hoot to go back and look at some of the star players' careers, including their time in the minor leagues.

The program is filled with interesting articles, such as a history of the Yankees and a recap of the previous season. A neat feature in the program is an 8x10 photograph of one of the Yankees. I've collected photographs of pitcher David Wells and former manager Billy Martin.

Cost: $3

Seats

It's going to be hard to go to the wrong seat, because there is only one way to enter the stadium and the signage is excellent. Also, they have ushers at every aisle. Their main job is to prevent people from going into the lower section, but they will also happily direct you to your seat. The field seats are further toward the end of the stadium than the rest. There are no bleachers here.

Shade

There is plenty of shade at Legends Field because the stadium is placed at an angle that puts the sun behind the stadium for a lot of the game. In addition, a large overhang covers most of the upper deck. What's tough to get here is a sunny seat. You'll get some sun if you sit in the lower level, but most of those seats are held by season ticket holders.

Food & Drink

Come hungry when you visit Legends Field. The food here made me think of the song from the Disney version of "Jack and the Beanstalk," where Goofy and Donald sing about the giant's feast. This is one stadium where everyone can find something they will like.

Let's start with the hot dogs. They were just about perfect. Even so, they were not the best offering here. This stadium has an Outback Steakhouse outlet. You won't be able to order a steak here, but you can get Outback's signature item, the delicious Bloomin' Onion. Their chicken fingers are also fantastic.

But don't stop your feast at the Outback. Travel on around the stadium and you will find just about everything you could want, including hot-boiled peanuts and deviled crab. The stadium also has a "Beers of the World" stand at both ends of the stadium. The world must be really small to New Yorkers because Corona was the only import I spotted, compared with nearly 40 at Clearwater's Beers of the World.

Souvenirs

If you want a souvenir, make sure you go to the store directly under the stairs that take you into the stadium. Sure there are places to go inside, but the biggest selection is in the store near the entrance. You'll find all the items that you could ask for — hats, t-shirts, playing cards, and other memorabilia, each one sporting Yankee pin stripes. There is also a wide selection of unique items. For instance, you can get a stuffed teddy bear in Yankee pin stripes or, if you want to spend a small fortune, a bat signed by Yankees star Derek Jeter. Just what every Yankees fan needs!

Autographs

Legends Field is not designed to be autograph friendly. In most stadiums, the best place to get an autograph is between the dugout and the end of the stadium. You will not be able to get into this area at Legend's Field unless you have a ticket for a lower reserved seat because the ushers guard every aisle and will not let you down. The only way you're going to get an autograph here is to wait by the practice field.

To get to the field, go to the ticket window and look to your right (as you face the window). You will see a walkway leading to the parking bridge. Next to the walkway is a grassy area that borders the practice fields. An eight-foot fence that players must walk by to get to the stadium surrounds the grassy area. Occasionally players will sign items that you toss to them over the fence. Call to them first to ask. Then if they OK it, toss your item over and they will sign it and toss it back.

Just don't expect to get a star to sign. The Yankees stars are as big a draw as the Beatles and rarely take the time to sign autographs. They would get swamped.

An even better vantage point, though it can get crowded, is the two bleachers overlooking the practice fields. To get to them, head toward the outside bathrooms and look for the walkway that leads to the bleachers. (It's easy to miss because landscaping hides the bleachers from most people.) Standing in the bleachers, you can get close to most of the superstars. If you're very lucky, you may get an autograph or two. Jason Giambi stood there for quite a while signing autographs over the fence the last time I was there.

A Game or an Experience?

Anytime you see the New York Yankees play, it is an experience. Well, maybe a circus. The Yankees do relatively little to entertain their fans other than play ball. There are between-inning trivia contests and I once saw the ground crew dancing to "YMCA." Except for opening day, when they pull out all the stops, you come to Legends Field for one thing: to see the Yankees play.

Up Close & Personal?

You're not going to get close to a Yankees player. Remember, this is the largest stadium in the Grapefruit League. Paradoxically, it is also one of the more compact. The stands extend only about halfway down the outfield line. That means the seating sections are quite high and are far from the playing field. The seats closest to the field are mostly held by season ticket holders. Unless you know one, you're not getting anywhere near the players during the game.

Getting Away

Count on delays. Tampa has some of the worst roads anywhere. There is always a traffic jam somewhere in the area, often several of them. The stadium is located on Dale Mabry Highway, a main thoroughfare in the Tampa area. Despite its six lanes, it is always congested. Figure you will have to wait and you won't be disappointed.

Before & After the Game: Restaurants

- Donatello, 232 North Dale Mabry Highway, Tampa; 813-875-6660
- Bern's Steak House, 1208 South Howard Avenue, Tampa; 813-251-2421
- Sidebern's, 2208 West Morrison Avenue, Tampa; 813-258-2233
- Sam Seltzers Steakhouse, 4744 North Dale Mabry Highway, Tampa; 813-873-7267
- Johnny Carino's, 1102 North Dale Mabry Highway, Tampa; 813-673-8700
- Fred Fleming's Famous BBQ, 217 Dale Mabry Highway South, Tampa; 813-875-3733
- Havana Village Sandwich Shop, 120 North Dale Mabry Highway, Tampa; 813-872-9049
- Matoi Sushi, 602 North Dale Mabry Highway, Tampa; 813-871-3237

Before & After the Game: Sports Bars

- Lee Roy Selmon's, 4302 West Boy Scout Boulevard, Tampa; 813-871-3287
- Press Box Sports, 222 South Dale Mabry Highway, Tampa; 813-876-3528

Before & After the Game: Attractions

For additional possibilities — and there are many — visit www.visittampabay.com, the web site of the Tampa Bay Convention and Visitors Bureau.

- Busch Gardens Africa, 3605 East Bougainvillea Avenue, Tampa; 888-800-5447, 813-987-5212, www.buschgardens.org

    Hours: Monday to Friday 10:00 a.m. to 6:00 p.m., Saturday and Sunday 9:00 a.m. to 7:00 p.m., but varies; call

    Admission: Adults $62, Children (3 to 9) $51.30, discounts for booking online

    This combination of theme park and wildlife park offers some of the best roller coasters in Florida. It also has wonderful animal exhibits, other rides, and live shows.

- Ybor City (www.ybor.org)
  Dubbed "Florida's Latin Quarter," Ybor City is a National Historic Landmark District packed with bars, restaurants, shops, and entertainment. The nation's first cigar factories were located here and you can still buy hand-rolled cigars in Ybor City's shops.
  A visitor's center for the district in located in The Centro Ybor Museum at 1600 East Eighth Avenue. It is open Monday to Saturday, 10:00 a.m. to 6:00 p.m. and Sundays noon to 6:00 p.m.
- Ybor City Museum State Park, 1818 East Ninth Avenue, Tampa; 813-247-6323, www.ybormuseum.org
  Hours: Daily 9:00 a.m. to 5:00 p.m., closed on major holidays
  Admission: Museum $3 (Children under 6 free)
  Includes an ornamental garden and a restored cigar worker's house. There are continuous cigar rolling demonstrations Fridays through Sundays from 9:30 a.m. to 1:00 p.m. A one-hour walking tour of the area and museum building is available Saturday at 10:30 a.m. for $6. Limited to 20, no reservations taken.
- Lowry Park Zoo, 1101 West Sligh Avenue, Tampa; 813-935-8552, www.lowryparkzoo.com
  Hours: Daily 9:30 a.m. to 5:00 p.m.; closed Thanksgiving and Christmas
  Admission: Adults $14.95, Seniors (60+) $13.95, Children (3 to 11) $10.50
  Florida wildlife, an assortment of primates, and exotic Asian species all call the zoo home. Highlights for kids include a petting zoo, an interactive area, and a Manatee Aquatic Center.
- MOSI (Museum of Science and Industry), 4801 East Fowler Avenue, Tampa; 813-987-6100, www.mosi.org
  Hours: Daily 9:00 a.m. to 5:00 p.m.
  Admission: Adults $19.95, Seniors (60+) $17.95, Children (2 to 12) $15.95
- Seminole Hard Rock Hotel & Casino Tampa, 5223 North Orient Road, Tampa; 800-282-7016, 813-627-7625

This joint project of the Seminole Tribe and Hard Rock Café International qualifies as both an attraction and a hotel. The casino offers bingo, slots, and low-stakes poker 24/7 to adults 18 and over. Parking is free. Kids are allowed in the casino restaurants with an adult parent or guardian, but they can't enter the gaming rooms.

Before & After the Game: Activities

- Tampa Bay Sportfishing Adventures, 558 14th Street, Palm Harbor; 727-784-0098
- Canoe Escape, Inc., 9335 East Fowler Avenue, Thonotosassa; 813-986-2067
- J.B. Starkey's Flatwoods Adventures, 12959 State Road 54, Odessa; 877-734-9453
- 18th Century Aviation (Ballooning), 11520 River Country Drive, Riverview; 813-969-3345
- DolphinQuest Eco Tours, The Florida Aquarium, 701 Channelside Drive, Tampa; 813-273-4000

Golf

- Tournament Players Club of Tampa Bay, 5300 West Lutz Lake Fern Road, Lutz; 866-PLAY-TPC, 813-949-0090
- Westchase Golf Club, 11602 Westchase Golf Drive, Tampa; 813-854-2331
- Saddlebrook Resort, 5700 Saddlebrook Way, Wesley Chapel; 813-973-1111
- Rocky Point Golf Course, 4151 Dana Shores Drive, Tampa; 813-673-4316
- Troon Golf at Innisbrook, The Westin Innisbrook Resort, 36750 U.S. Highway 19 North, Palm Harbor; 727-942-2000
- Heritage Harbor, 19502 Heritage Harbor Parkway, Lutz; 813-949-4886

Hotels Near the Ballpark

- Days Inn Airport / Stadium, 2522 North Dale Mabry Highway, Tampa; 813-877-6181

- Holiday Inn Express Hotel Suites / Stadium Airport, 4750 North Dale Mabry Highway, Tampa; 813-877-6061
- Hilton Tampa Airport Westshore, 2225 North Lois Avenue, Tampa; 813-877-6688
- Quorum Tampa Westshore, 700 North Westshore Boulevard, Tampa; 813-289-8200
- DoubleTree Tampa Westshore Airport Hotel, 4500 West Cypress Street, Tampa; 813-879-4800
- Hampton Inn Tampa Airport Westshore, 4817 West Laurel Street, Tampa; 813-287-0778
- Sheraton Suites Tampa Airport, 4400 West Cypress Street, Tampa; 813-873-8675
- Tampa Westshore Marriott, 1001 North Westshore Boulevard, Tampa; 813-287-2555

Chapter 14

Philadelphia Phillies Bright House Networks Field

Clearwater

While many fans of Spring Training enjoyed the antique feel of Jack Russell Stadium, the Phillies Spring Training home for 57 years, they can all say good riddance because Clearwater has found just about the perfect mix of new and old at its new park, Bright House Networks Field. This is the first completely new park that has been able to merge the old-time feel with the new amenities required by the modern era of baseball. Simply put, it is a great ballpark. It's not too big and it has lots of quirky aspects that put it in the top two or three parks in the league. In fact, the only drawback here is the parking. The non-reserved lot is down the street from the front entrance, a good 15-minute walk from the stadium. Still, the walk is well worth it if you are a baseball fan.

The positives start at the front entrance. The Spanish architecture and fountains are architecturally appealing. Better yet, the practice field is located right to the left of the ticket window. While waiting for the gates to open, you can look down at pitchers practicing their fielding skills. Just don't linger too long because you'll want to get inside and walk around to experience the park to its fullest.

The first thing you'll notice as you walk in is your view of the main field. Unlike in every other Grapefruit League ballpark — most of which force you to walk through tunnels to get to the main seating area — the main concourse here is

Photo by Kelly Monaghan.

located above the seats. That means you can see the field and the game no matter where you are in the stadium.

If you turn to the left after entering, you'll find a "Beers of the World" stand, stocked with over 40 different types of beer. A little further along, you'll see the kids' playground and moonwalk, great touches that only a couple of other parks offer. Towards the stands, there is a picnic table area on a tiered terrace. This is often filled with groups, but you can buy a ticket specifically for this section and watch the game from the terrace.

You'll see something else unique to Bright House Networks Field as you walk around: the berm goes completely around the outfield. In all other Grapefruit League parks with berms, the berm is limited to one section of the outfield. Here, you can sit over either the right or left field wall. Adding to the excitement, the bullpens are cut into the left field berm; so you can stand on the berm and watch the pitchers warm up at closer range than at any other park in the league.

As you make your way around the park, you'll also spot a variety of concessions ranging from the typical to the extra special — in this case, the cheese steak. There's only one stand that sells this Philly treat and the lines get quite long. Join the line; it's a "don't miss" specialty.

With just 7,000 seats, Bright House Network Fields is fairly intimate, and there isn't a bad seat in the house. Even the top row is OK. But if you're seated there and want to get closer to the action, you can move to the berm.

The planners did a particularly good job with the outfield seats. In most parks, the designers want to pack in as many seats as possible, which means that the outfield seats face center field. As a result, you get a killer neck ache from having to turn your head to watch the game. Not so at Bright House Networks Field. The outfield seats here are angled toward second base, and you are looking straight at the center of the game. No turning or neck ache involved.

The most unusual seats in the house are found at the tiki bar at the end of the left field line. Jack Russell Stadium had a tiki bar that offered just a few seats around a small bar. The new stadium has supersized it, with 75 seats around a massive bar, complete with televisions and full liquor service. Right below the bar is a tiered section of high barstools facing the field that seats 100 more. Seating in this area is first-come, first-served and there is a server to bring you drinks from the bar. It's a really great touch.

Bright House Network Fields has also avoided the biggest drawback of most new parks: the lack of autograph opportunities for the fans. Typically, the new parks minimize fan contact with players by allowing the players to enter and leave the field through the dugouts. Remarkably, Clearwater's stadium planners have forced the Phillies to walk by the crowd all the way from their dugout to past the picnic tables to get to their clubhouse. This allows for perfect signing opportunities all along the third base side, with the best at the end of the picnic area.

Getting visitor autographs is tougher. Unlike the Phillies, visitors walk through their dugout to get to and from the field. Still, you are allowed to get near the field here, and when you do, you can often get visitors to sign for you.

Maybe it's the fact that Phillies Spring Training and Clearwater have been synonymous since 1948. But whatever the reason, Clearwater has got it right.

Fast Facts

Bright House Networks Field
601 Old Coachman Road
Clearwater, FL 33765
727-442-8496
http://philadelphia.phillies.mlb.com
http://www.philliesspringtraining.com/

Getting There

Take U.S. 19 to Drew Street (SR 590). It's just north of Gulf to Bay Boulevard (SR 60). Turn west onto Drew. The stadium is about a quarter mile ahead, on the right.

Parking

In a stadium where so much is right, it's amazing the parking can be so wrong. The "premium" parking lot ($10) is near the park, but it is small and fills up fast. The general parking lot is farther away from the stadium than any other parking lot in the league. Depending on whether you park in the front of the lot or the back, you'll have to walk through the unpaved lot, down a road, and through the reserved spaces to get to the stadium. It's a 10- to 15-minute walk in the sun. Be prepared.

Cost: $5 to $10

Tickets

Bright House Networks Field has been a difficult ticket to get in the past and given its amenities, chances are it will be equally difficult in the future. The average attendance tends to be over 7,000, and the park has only 7,000 fixed seats. So buy your tickets early. In most cases, you'll get into the game if you wait to buy until game day, but you'll want to bring a blanket or get to the game early because you'll be in general admission or on the berm.

If you don't feel close enough, you can move to the berm and enjoy the game from there.

Capacity: 8,500 (including berm)
Average Attendance: 7,025

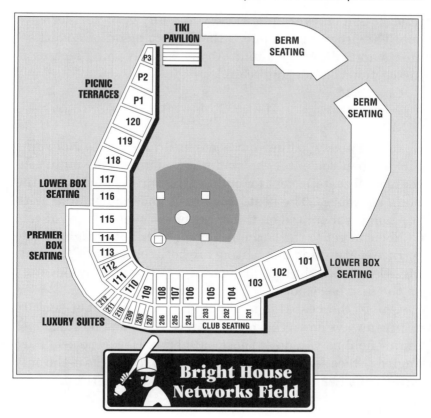

Ticket Prices:
> Club Level $25
> Premium Box $19
> Field Box $17
> Picnic Terrace $15
> Berm $9

For Tickets: 727-442-8496

Programs

Don't miss the Phillies' program. It is one of the League's best. It contains plenty of articles and statistics, mug shots of the players, and items from the Philadelphia Phillies' historical archives. The lengthy section on the Phillies players is presented in numerical order — making it easy to identify the players. The section includes selected statistics and personal information on every player, so you really get a feel for each one. The program has about the perfect blend of advertisements and editorial content. About the only thing lacking is instructions on keeping score.

Cost: $3

Seats

It's very easy to find your seats at Bright House Networks Field. When you enter the stadium, you are on the main concourse. All seats, except for club seating, are located below the main concourse. The seats are broad and comfortable, with cup holders mounted on the backs of the seat in front of you.

You can get to the berm by going either left or right, while terrace seating and bar seating are both to the left. Club seating is located on the second floor. To get to it, take the elevators on the first base side.

One of the best things about the park is that if you are sitting a ways down the outfield lines, you won't be staring at center field as you do at most ballparks. Here, the seats are angled to face second base. Bright House Networks is the only Grapefruit League ballpark where you will find this.

Shade

The stadium has a large roof and is situated perfectly for both those who want a sunburn and those who don't. For those who don't, try and get a ticket in sections 108 to 116. If you want to burn, go lay out on the berm and soak up the rays. Other seats get a mix of sun and shade as the day progresses.

Food & Drink

The concessionaires at Bright House Networks Field did not let me down. There are three large concession stands, each offering the traditional array of baseball food. The hot dogs are thick and juicy here, but the must-try gems are the specialty items, particularly the cheese steak sandwich. Don't miss this perfect mix of grilled steak, onions, and melted cheese. It is absolutely fantastic. You'll find it at the stand behind home plate.

Also, don't miss the "Beers of the World" stand located on

the third base side of the stadium. It offers over 40 different types of beers, mostly bottled. It also sells beers by the bucket, five beers at a discounted price. The variety is a welcome relief from the Bud, Coors, and Miller offered by most Florida stadiums.

Finally, the stadium provides the largest tiki bar I've ever seen at a ballpark. It seats 75 people, and every seat has a view of the playing field. The bar stays open after the game. It's a good place to hang out while the parking lot clears, particularly if you have a designated driver.

Souvenirs

The souvenir stands are adequate. Diamond Outfitters is located near the front entrance with a smaller stand on the first base side of the park. You'll find the usual shirts, hats, and baseballs here, including merchandise with the logo of Clearwater's minor league team, the Thrashers. The only unique Phillies item I've seen on my visits was a DVD dedicated to the team's history in its old stadium in Philadelphia,

Photo by Kelly Monaghan.

The berm at Bright House Networks Field gives baseball fans space to get comfortable, relax, and enjoy themselves.

which, like Jack Russell Stadium, was torn down in 2003.

To get to the store, turn left immediately after you enter the stadium. If you like to shop, come early. The store gets crowded as gametime nears. You may even have to wait in line to get in.

Autographs

Whenever a new Grapefruit League stadium opens, the autograph opportunities seem to disappear. That isn't the case at this stadium. In fact, the autograph opportunities are actually better at Bright House Networks Field than they were at the old Jack Russell Stadium. While it's not the easiest place to get autographs, it offers better than average opportunities to get your favorite Philly's signature.

The best place to get autographs is at the far corner of the Picnic 1 section. This area offers players who stop to sign some protection from flying baseballs, a key to getting them to stay awhile. Every Philly, as he walks back to the clubhouse, must pass this corner. Of course some players, like star Pat Burrell, sprint past to avoid autograph seekers, but then some players go out of their way to avoid signing no matter what park they are in. Another good area is the wall between the dugout and the end of the first base line. Players walk the wall and are often willing to come over and sign for fans who wait there.

For visitors' autographs, hang out on either side of the dugout and hope. Visiting players can leave the field through the dugout, so it's easy for them to avoid fans.

A Game or an Experience?

Any new park is an experience, but this one is a cut above the rest. There are so many surprises and fun experiences at Bright House Networks Field, that you get far more than a game. Whether you choose to enjoy a margarita at the tiki bar, let your kid loose in the kiddie play area, or sit on the grass next to the bullpen on a massive berm, you're going to get your money's worth here. There are also contests that anyone can enter. On my last visit, my favorite was the Kane's Furniture Best Seat in the House contest. Anyone who bought a program could enter by filling out a form and dropping it in a box before the end of the first inning. At that time, they drew a name and that person and a guest got to sit in leather recliners at the top of the section right behind home plate. I only wish I had won.

Up Close & Personal

This stadium is surprisingly intimate, with only 7,000 fixed seats — a relatively low number for a Spring Training stadium. You'll feel fairly close to the action in any of them. In addition, there are wonderful areas that let you get closer to players than you can at almost any other park in the league. For instance, go to the berm and stand next to the bullpen. When the pitchers warm up, they will be less than a yard from you, and you can listen to everything the coach and player say to each other.

Also, behind the visitors' dugout, they have cut away a section of the stands to allow you to watch the players as they exit or enter the stadium. It's a view you won't find elsewhere.

Getting Away

Leaving the stadium isn't easy. First of all, you have the long walk back to your car. Then, there are only a couple of exits from the parking lot onto a three-lane street. Then you have to turn onto Drew Street, which is not a major artery. It's not until you get onto U.S. 19 that you can finally move more than a few miles per hour.

Before & After the Game: Restaurants

- Joe's Crab Shack, 2730 Gulf to Bay Boulevard, Clearwater; 727-799-8530

Before & After the Game: Sports Bars

- Hooters Restaurants – Clearwater, 2800 Gulf to Bay Boulevard, Clearwater; 727-797-4008
- Pete & Shorty's, 2820 Gulf to Bay Boulevard, Clearwater; 727-799-0580
- Beef 'O'Brady's, 1500 McMullen Booth Road, Clearwater; 727-725-4023

Before & After the Game: Attractions

Note: Attractions listed in Chapters 13, 16, and 17 are also within striking distance. While there's some overlap below, you may want to check the other chapters before deciding what to do, especially if you are spending a few days in the area. For more options, consult www.floridasbeach.com, web site of the St. Petersburg-Clearwater Convention and Visitors Bureau.

- Captain Memo's Original Pirate Cruise, 25 Causeway Boulevard, Dock 3, Clearwater Beach; 727-446-2587, www.captmemo.com
  Hours: Daily 10:00 a.m., 2:00 p.m., and sunset (6:00 p.m. in March)
  Cost: Adults $32 ($35 evening), Seniors (65+) $27, Juniors (13 to 17) $27, Children $22
  Explore the Gulf on a two-hour cruise from the Clearwater Marina. Champagne is served on the evening cruise.

- Celebration Station, 24546 U.S. Highway 19 North, Clearwater; 727-791-1799
  Hours: Sunday to Thursday noon to 9:00 p.m., Friday noon to midnight, and Saturday 10:00 a.m. to midnight
  Cost: Varies
  Family-oriented mini-theme park with go-karts, bumper boats, games, miniature golf, batting cages, shows, and dining.

- Derby Lane, 10490 Gandy Boulevard North, St. Petersburg; 727-812-3339, www.derbylane.com
  Hours: Monday to Saturday, January to mid June. Gates open daily at 6:30 p.m., post at 7:30 p.m. and Monday, Wednesday, and Saturday gates open ay 11:30 a.m. and post at 12:30 p.m.
  Admission: $1 general admission
  Greyhounds race here nightly except Sunday during Spring Training season. General parking is free, or let the valet do it for $3. There's an all-you-can-eat buffet nightly (reservations suggested). If you tire of the dogs, you can play cards in the Poker Room until midnight.
  Note: You must be 12 or older to enter and 18 or older for admission to the card room.

Before & After the Game: Activities

- Moccasin Lake Nature Park, 2750 Park Trail Lane; Clearwater, 727-462-6024
  Hours: Tuesday to Friday 9:00 a.m. to 5:00 p.m., Saturday and Sunday 10:00 a.m. to 6:00 p.m. Closed Monday unless it is a legal holiday.
  Admission: Adults $3, Children (3 to 12) $2
  Look and listen for nocturnal creatures on a special two-hour walk with a park guide. The park offers an environmental and energy education center along with a lake, upland forest, wetlands, and lots of native plant and animal species. A one-mile nature trail winds through the park. The Interpretive Center features wildlife exhibits, displays, and information.
  Note: The park holds regular Night Hikes on the second Wednesday of every month. Hikes start at 7:00 p.m. in March. The fee for these guided two-hour walks is $3.50 for adults and $2.50 for children 3 to 12.

Fishing

- Queen Fleet, 25 Causeway Boulevard, #52 and #53, Clearwater Beach; 727-446-7666
- Reef Tours, 3334 Crab Trap Lane, Hudson; 727-410-5551
- Charter Boat Two C's II, Slip 27 Municipal Marina, Clearwater Beach; 727-797-0784

Golf

- Airco Golf Course, 13690 Stonybrook Drive, Clearwater; 727-573-4653
- Bardmoor Golf Course, 8001 Cumberland Road, Largo; 727-392-1234
- Cypress Links at Mangrove Bay, 875 62nd Avenue Northeast, St. Petersburg; 727-551-3333
- Pasadena Yacht & Country Club, 6300 Pasadena Point Boulevard South, Gulfport; 727-381-7922
- Wentworth Golf Club, 2990 Wentworth Way, Tarpon Springs; 727-942-4760

Hotels Near the Ballpark

- Hampton Inn Clearwater, 21030 U.S. Highway 19 North, Clearwater; 727-797-8173
- Radisson Clearwater Central, 20967 U.S. Highway 19 North, Clearwater; 727-799-1181
- Quality Inn, 20162 U.S. Highway 19 North, Clearwater; 727-799-6133
- Fairfield Inn & Suites, 3070 Gulf to Bay Boulevard, Clearwater; 727-724-6223
- Clearwater Inn, 21252 U.S. Highway 19 North, Clearwater; 727-799-1569
- La Quinta, 21338 U.S. Highway 19 North, Clearwater; 727-799-1565

Hotels on the Beach

- Quality Hotel on the Beach, 655 South Gulfview Boulevard, Clearwater Beach; 800-228-5151, 727-442-7171

Chapter 15

Pittsburgh Pirates
McKechnie Field

Bradenton

McKechnie Field is hidden away in a corner of Bradenton, well off the beaten path. It's worth looking for, however, because when you find it, you'll be pleased. Everything seems to be a little better here than at most Spring Training sites. The grass is greener, the people friendlier, the stadium prettier, and the atmosphere livelier. Perhaps that's because many people in the town are personally invested in making McKechnie Field one of the best Spring Training sites in baseball.

The stadium, which had a major renovation in 1992, has been on the same site since 1923, and the Pirates have been training in Bradenton for 36 years. Together, the two are woven into the fabric of the town. In fact, McKechnie's local booster club raised the money for the renovations, and its 120 members run the stadium on a volunteer basis. There's no need for tax dollars here. The townsfolk feel strongly enough about keeping baseball in their backyard that they pitch in to do the job themselves. That makes McKechnie Field an extra special place.

The park is quaint, evoking images of stadiums long gone. There's no big wall around the stands and playing field. Instead, the roof and stadium are made of exposed metal beams painted green. When you walk inside, you're treated to one of the friendliest staffs you'll find anywhere, thanks again to the booster club. The stadium has few employees; nearly everyone working here is a booster club member and volunteer.

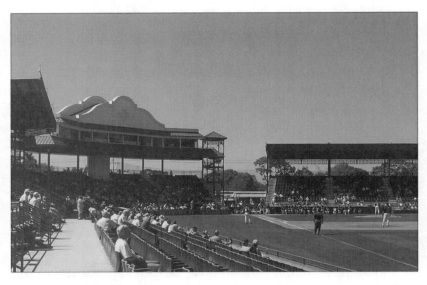

Photo by Kelly Monaghan.

They're easy to spot in their yellow polo shirts. All 120 members seem to pitch in.

Despite its average size, McKechnie Field is one of the most intimate ballparks in the Grapefruit League, thanks to efforts of the booster club. After the stadium was renovated in 1992, the boosters looked at it and decided that the front row was too far from the diamond. They raised enough money to add several rows down front to bring the action closer to the fans.

In addition, this ballpark gives you wonderful behind-the-scenes access. You can stand next to the team's batting cages and watch players practicing and being coached. You can stand two feet from the bullpen to watch the Pirates' pitchers warm up and hear the pop of a fastball in the catcher's mitt. You can watch the players work out in a small courtyard by their clubhouse (at the end of the stadium on the first base side). I noticed that many used nontraditional items, such as a bungee cord, as they prepared for the game. I even watched a worker cleaning the team's shoes. He would take a pair, polish it, work the grass from the player's cleats, and then line the shoes up for the player to pick up.

This is a good park for home-team autographs. To get them, head for the end of the stadium on the first base side. Every player has to walk past this area through a section about 20 feet wide. Players have to go out of their way to avoid signing here and most will give you an autograph.

There are two serious drawbacks to McKechnie Field, and they both involve the seating. First, these seats are the most uncomfortable of any stadium I have ever visited. They remind me of a McDonald's booster seat — small and made of hard plastic. The inflexibility of the structure and material forces you to sit at a 90-degree angle. If you have any girth at all to your backside, you will probably not fit into them. Save yourself the pain and sit in the bleachers. The only relief comes in the form of a seat cushion that the stadium rents out. It's only a dollar, and it's well worth every cent. There's no such easy fix for the other problem. In addition to the hard plastic, you will suffer from an obstructed view if you get an aisle seat near the top of the reserved sections. Poles similar to those found at Fenway Park in Boston partially block your view.

Tip: The Box Office won't mention the obstructed view when you buy tickets. So be sure you ask before you pay.

While those two flaws are significant, they do not erase McKechnie Field's many charms. In fact, it offers the best value in baseball for my money. It has the cheapest reserved seats in the League, by several dollars, plus great atmosphere. I highly recommend incorporating a visit here into any Spring Training vacation. Just remember to buy bleacher seats if you want room to spread out.

Fast Facts

McKechnie Field
1611 9th Street West
Bradenton, FL 34205
941-748-4610
http://pittsburgh.pirates.mlb.com

Getting There

Take I-75 to Exit 220, Route 64. Go west on 64 to 9th Street West. Turn left to the stadium. It's less than a mile ahead at the corner of 17th Avenue West.

Parking

Parking lot? What parking lot? McKechnie Field is in the middle of town. You're on your own here. But don't fret. Most of the businesses in the area open their parking lots up to fans on game days, for a fee. The closer you park, the more you pay. If you park in the lot of the restaurant next door to the stadium, you'll pay $10.

Caution: Avoid parking across the main highway on the west side of the stadium. Cars parked there are in the direct line of balls that fly out of the stadium. A baseball can put a nasty ding into a car and break the windshield. Several cars got whacked during the game I attended.

Cost: Variable

Tickets

You'll almost certainly be able to get tickets to any game you like because the park virtually never sells out. There are over 1,500 tickets left on the average game day. The supply tightens when the Red Sox and Yankees come in to play, but there are tickets available on game day even then. The top-attended games in 2004, for instance, missed selling out by nearly 600 tickets.

With its great atmosphere and low ticket prices, you'd expect seats to be hard to get. But Bradenton is a bit out of the way, the seats are uncomfortable, and the Pirates aren't a marquee team.

Capacity: 6,562
Average Attendance: 4,971
Ticket Prices:
 Box Seats $9
 Reserved $8
 Reserved Bleacher $6
For Tickets: 941-748-4610

Programs

The Pirates have one of the cheaper programs in the Grapefruit League and also one of the best. It is printed on thick glossy paper and has all the essentials — mug shots,

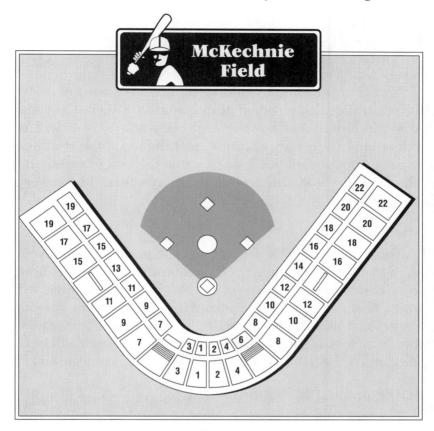

statistics, and scorecard. In addition to these, the copy I got had a number of interesting stories ranging from a review of the past season to a history of Pirates baseball in Bradenton, along with the *Baseball America* prospect sheet. Don't miss this program.

Cost: $3

Seats

Finding your seat here isn't hard, particularly since you won't be left to do it on your own. One of the corps of very friendly volunteers (look for the yellow polo shirt) will point you in the right direction. Still, when you enter the stadium, you may find it confusing at first glance because there are wide gaps between the sections. Bear in mind that there are only three types of seats: The box seats are below the main seating aisle, the reserved are above, and the bleachers are on either side of the stadium at the ends of each foul line. You can't miss the bleachers; they are silver metal; everything else is yellow and green.

A word of warning. In most stadiums, box seats are below the main aisle and reserved grandstands are above the aisle. At McKechnie, not all box seats are below the main aisle. The tops of boxes 1 to 4 are all the way at the top of the stadium. I speak from experience; I was excited to get a box seat and when I got to the stadium, I was second row from the top. Very disappointing.

Shade

This is a pretty shady stadium. The grandstands have a large roof that covers most of the seats, and the sun is behind the stadium for most of the game. But if you want sun, don't worry, there's plenty of that, too. Sit in the first few rows of the grandstands or better yet, the reserved bleachers, where there's no roof. If you sit on the right side, your back will be to the sun; on the left field side, you'll be sideways to the sun.

Food & Drink

There are plenty of concession stands at McKechnie Field. As you walk in, you'll spot one near the entrance, complete with picnic tables and a grassy area. Others are located down the first and third base sides of the main concourse and under the main grandstands at the center of the stadium.

Unfortunately, a lot of concession stands doesn't add up to a lot of variety. There is nothing here that you can't get at other stadiums. The hot dogs are nondescript, just your basic hot dog. The pizza sold at the stand under the main grandstands is locally made but not quite as good as the pizza at most neighborhood pizza joints.

Souvenirs

Most of the merchandise here is in one small store, but there seems to be a ton of offerings. They range from typical ballpark souvenirs to a mini monster truck, an item unique to McKechnie Field. The store is directly to the right of the main entrance and can be accessed from both inside and outside the stadium. If you come in from inside the stadium, make sure you get your hand stamped by the volunteer at the door for easy reentry to the stadium.

The stadium also sells a limited selection of souvenirs from two merchandise carts. They are located on the third base side of the stadium near the front entrance.

Tip: Shop early at the store; it gets busy quickly.

Autographs

This is a pretty easy place to get autographs, at least from the Pirates players. Walk to the end of the stadium on the first base side. You will come to a handicapped access ramp with a railing on it. The bleachers are on the other side. If you wait by the ramp, you're going to get several autographs. An even surer bet is to move to the very end of the ramp nearest the field. Every player must walk by that point on the way from clubhouse to field. You're so close to them here that players have to go out of their way to ignore your request for an autograph. Most sign.

Note: It helps to know the players' names and faces in advance, because there are times you will have to call them over.

Getting visitors' autographs is not that difficult if the players are willing. On the third base side, hidden from the seats, is a fence that goes to the visitors' clubhouse. All visitors must walk by this fence to get to the lockers. Deciding to sign is up to them.

A Game or an Experience?

Just going to such a quaint park is a winning experience. That's fortunate because the stadium does little to increase the entertainment value of attending a game here. There are no mid-inning contests or games. If you want a little extra excitement, check out the batting cages near the end of the first base side. Players head there before and after the game to work on their skills, and you're welcome to watch.

The team does offer a couple of extras for kids. There is a blowup moonwalk for small children and a pitching area for bigger children.

At Spring Training parks like McKechnie Field, fans get close to the action and up close and personal with their favorite personalities. Above right, the team's mascot greets visitors. Below, players relax and warm up for the game.

Photos by Kelly Monaghan.

Up Close & Personal?

If you sit up near the front of the grandstands at McKechnie Field you will be sure to feel like you're part of the game. This is quite simply the closest you are going to get to a baseball game without actually being a player.

In contrast, the top of the bleachers is a good distance from the action, and you face center field if you look straight ahead. However, these seats are the exception, not the rule at this stadium. There are few other seats where you won't feel on top of the action here.

Getting Away

While finding the stadium can be an issue, leaving it is not. A four-lane highway runs by the edge of McKechnie Field, allowing for a quick exodus. In addition, because there is no central parking lot at this stadium, you will not have to wait in line behind a bunch of other cars to get out of the parking area and onto the road.

Before & After the Game: Restaurants

- Anna Maria Oyster Bar, 6906 14th Street West, Bradenton; 941-758-7880
- Corner Cafe, 548 12th Street West, Bradenton; 941-747-1277
- Chili's Grill & Bar, 3715 Desoto Junction, Bradenton; 941-747-1893
- First Watch, 8306 Market Street, Bradenton; 941-907-6657
- Popi's Place, 818 17th Avenue West, Bradenton; 941-746-7078

Before & After the Game: Sports Bars

- Beef 'O'Brady's, 6703 Manatee Avenue West, Bradenton; 941-761-1444

Before & After the Game: Attractions

For more ideas on what to do while you're in the immediate area, be sure to visit www.flagulfislands.com, the Bradenton

Area Convention and Visitors Bureau web site.

Note: The Tampa Bay region is loaded with attractions and activities of all sorts. For more ideas about things to do in this part of the state, the attractions listed in Chapters 13, 14, 16, and 17 are all within 40 to 60 miles of Bradenton, or about 60 to 90 minutes away.

- South Florida Museum and Parker Manatee Aquarium, 201 10th Street West, Bradenton; 941-746-4131, www.southfloridamuseum.org

  Hours: Monday to Saturday 10:00 a.m. to 5:00 p.m., Sunday noon to 5:00 p.m.

  Admission: Adults $13.75, Seniors (60+) $11.75, Children (4 to 12) $8.75

  The collection at this museum highlights the region's natural history and the cultures and artifacts of Florida Native Americans. Visitors interested in manatees will want to explore the museum's Parker Manatee Aquarium, where they can meet Snooty, the resident manatee. If the subject interests you, be sure to check out the manatee program that is offered several times each day.

Before & After the Game: Activities

Golf

- Legacy Golf Club, 8255 Legacy Boulevard, Bradenton; 941-907-7920
- Rosedale Golf & Country Club, 5100 87th Street East, Bradenton; 941-756-0004
- The River Club, 6600 River Club Boulevard, Bradenton; 941-751-4211

Hotels Near the Ballpark

- Days Inn, 3506 First Street West, Bradenton; 941-746-1141
- Comfort Inn, 580 East 66th Street Circle East, Bradenton; 941-747-7500
- Holiday Inn Riverfront, 100 Riverfront Drive West, Bradenton; 941-747-3727

- Holiday Inn Express, 648 67th Street Circle East, Bradenton; 941-748-6610
- Quality Inn & Suites, 2303 First Street East, Bradenton; 941-747-6465

Photo courtesy of Roger Dean Stadium.

Wacky contests and pageantry are part of the fun at many Grapefruit League stadiums. Above, a song contest at Jupiter's Roger Dean Stadium. Below, a color guard assembles under the March sun at Tampa's Legends Field.

Photo by Kelly Monaghan.

Chapter 16

Tampa Bay Devil Rays
Progress Energy Park
at Al Lang Field in St. Petersburg

No stadium in the Grapefruit League has a better location than Progress Energy Park. From the grandstands, you can watch sailboats come in and out of Tampa Bay. Before the game, you can walk along the water's edge or visit several St. Petersburg attractions — all without moving your car. After the game, there are lots of restaurants and bars to sate your hunger and thirst, and they're all within walking distance.

If only the stadium lived up to its surroundings. This is a tired old park that looks as if it needs a heavy face-lift, or at least a paint job. It is, in my opinion, the worst place to watch a Spring Training game in Florida.

That's not to say that it's all bad here. Progress Energy Park is a good place to get an autograph. The trivia contests held between innings are fun for spectators and participants — and award the best prizes in the Grapefruit League. And die-hard fans will enjoy the sign on the concourse that relates the long history of baseball in St. Petersburg, a place where Babe Ruth once swung his bat.

Still, what you'll most likely remember are the unofficial guests who pay nothing to watch the game and always arrive near the end of the seventh inning. Those guests are flocks and flocks of seagulls. Now, don't misunderstand, there are seagulls at plenty of Florida ballparks. There are just a whole heck of a lot more seagulls at Progress Energy Park.

Near the beginning of the game, a few gulls hang out in the

Photo by Robert Rogers.

outfield, moving only when a ball comes near. They'll even dive bomb a player or two, which is quite a spectacle. Come the end of the seventh inning, the gulls must send out some sort of signal. Hundreds more suddenly appear and fly into the stands to pick up all the dropped hot dogs, peanuts, and other morsels.

But the seagulls aren't the problem. The problem is the stadium itself. First, it is facing the absolute worst direction for a Spring Training ballpark, south and west. Nearly everyone is in the sun at some point in the game, and most people will have the sun in their face for at least half the game. Second, the stadium is cement. They didn't bother painting it for some reason. Maybe they were cutting costs. However, this stadium was built in 1976. There must have been some money available for paint at some point during the past 31 years. One coat of paint couldn't cost that much.

Third, the souvenirs and concessions are the least inspiring of any in Florida. There is nothing here that can't be found anyplace else.

The best reasons for coming to a game at Al Lang Field are to collect autographs and to see the marquee teams that come in to play the Devil Rays. Unlike at most other Spring Training ballparks, ticket availability for games with marquee teams is virtually guaranteed here.

Fast Facts

Progress Energy Park, home of Al Lang Field
230 First Street South
St. Petersburg, FL 33701
727-825-3250
http://tampabay.devilrays.mlb.com
http://www.stpete.org/allang.htm

Getting There

Take I-275 to Exit 22, I-175. Continue straight (east) as I-175 turns into Fifth Avenue South. Turn left at First Street South. The stadium is three blocks ahead on your right, at Second Avenue Southeast.

Parking

The main parking lot is right next to the stadium. You really can't get any closer to a ballpark than this lot. Still, if you get to the game early, I recommend parking at the St. Petersburg Pier instead. It is a very pleasant walk to the stadium, along the water and through a public park. And it puts you in the perfect place if you want to enjoy a night on the town.

Cost: $5 stadium, pier free on a space available basis

Tickets

This is the easiest ticket to get in Spring Training. After all, the Tampa Bay Devil Rays play 82 regular season games about 10 blocks down the road from Progress Energy Park. The team has a hard time selling out regular season games, much less exhibitions.

Overall, the stadium averages about three-quarters full for any given game. Even when the Yankees play here, they rarely sell out.

One nice place to sit here is the small berm area on the first base side. It puts you close to the players because the bench for the Devil Rays' bullpen is along the front of the berm. Tickets for it are available only on the day of the game, but you don't need a berm ticket to sit there. You can get to it even if your seat is elsewhere in the stadium.

Capacity: 6,557
Average Attendance: 4,717
Ticket Prices:
Field Boxes $19
Loge Boxes $16
Grandstand $14
General Admission Berm $7
For Tickets: 727-825-3250

Programs

The Devil Rays have no Spring Training program. You can purchase a scorecard that includes a roster, but nothing else. There are no instructions on how to keep score, so if you are one of the many who do not know this art, save the buck.

Cost: $1

Seats

It's not hard to find your seat at Progress Energy Park. The box seats are below the main seating aisle and the reserved seats above. The berm areas are past the ends of the grandstands on both sides of the ballpark. The stadium is well marked and has plenty of ushers to assist you. Besides, at most games you can choose just about any seat. There are plenty available.

Shade

You will get burned here if you do not bring sunscreen. The stadium is situated so that, with the exception of a very few seats that are shaded by the roof, the sun cooks all fans fairly evenly. The first base stands face the sun for the first half of the game, the third base stands, for the second half. It's the only stadium in the Grapefruit League with this alignment. Obviously, someone didn't do his or her homework.

Food & Drink

You're not going to find anything imaginative here, just the typical baseball fare of hot dogs, peanuts, and beer. There are regular and "foot-long" hotdogs, which live up to their billing, as well as Italian sausages available from concessionaires.

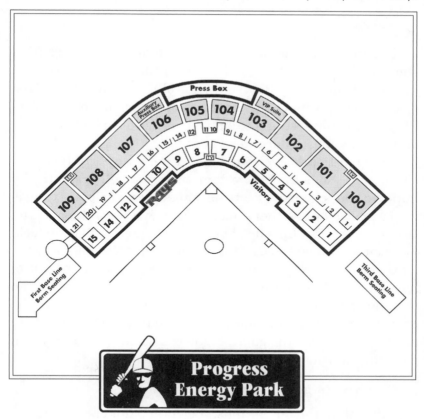

On the plus side there are some unusual beers available, like Boddington Ale, a deep, golden-colored brew all the way from Manchester, England.

Souvenirs

You will find souvenirs at stands near the center of the stadium on the main concourse. One stand carries the basics, the other has a better selection of the more expensive items. There's nothing very imaginative at either one, but you'll be able to get a t-shirt, hat, or logoed ball. Outside by the box office, a garage sale-type table also offers souvenirs.

If you get there early, you might be able to snag a free souvenir by hanging around outside the outfield walls, not too far from the parking lot, during batting practice. You'll have company, but if you're nimble you should be able to snag a free ball or two. Last time I was there, one guy had amassed seven!

Autographs

The autograph possibilities are the main attraction at this stadium. You have a good shot at getting autographs from just about any Devil Ray you want plus any member of the visiting team. One of the reasons is the lack of competition. Players are more willing to sign when there isn't a big crowd, and that's almost guaranteed here.

As at most parks, you will want to get here early. If you arrive a couple of hours before gametime, you will dramatically improve your chances of getting signatures. The place to go is the outfield side of either dugout. The Devil Rays' dugout is on the first base side. Line up along the wall, and you'll be in luck. For visitors' autographs, do the same on the third base side.

If you don't get to the stadium early, you won't be out of luck but it will be more difficult. Wait until the game is over, then go to the berm area on the first base side. Stand in the corner closest to the stadium. Many Devil Rays go to the outfield and work out after the game. Some will come over to this area after they finish.

A Game or an Experience?

Other than the autographs, the entertainment during the game is the best thing going for Progress Energy Park. Once the game gets underway, there are contests before every inning. That's more than in any other ballpark. Better yet, these aren't your traditional contests, such as spinning around on a bat or running to a goal. They consist of trivia questions and similar games. My personal favorite was a "name that tune" contest. Best of all, the team does not just give out gift certificates or a t-shirt. Most of the prizes are memorabilia autographed by the Devil Rays' stars.

Up Close & Personal?

If you want to be close to a baseball player, step out to the berm and sit on the front row. The berm is directly behind the Devil Rays' bullpen and there are plenty of players around.

Note: Be aware that players aren't willing to talk during the game and won't sign autographs while they're in the bullpen.

In any other spot, you will be quite separated from the players, thanks to the stadium's design. While Progress Energy Park has an average number of seats, the stadium stops shortly after the first and third bases. There are no bleachers stretching out alongside the outfield lines, which is what allows every seat to be close to the field in the better-designed stadiums. Here, the top seats are relatively high up and the front row seats are separated from the field by a four-foot cement wall. You have to look over it to watch the game.

Getting Away

It's easy to get back on the road from Progress Energy Park. For one thing, there aren't that many people here, so getting out of the lot is a relatively speedy process. For another, St. Pete has some of the least congested roads in Florida. Once you're out of the parking lot, you're quickly back on the Interstate.

Before & After the Game: Restaurants

- Fourth Street Shrimp Store Restaurant, 1006 4th Street North, St. Petersburg; 727-822-0325
- Dan Marino's Town Tavern, 121 2nd Avenue North, St. Petersburg; 727-822-4413
- Central Avenue Seafood & Oyster Bar, 249 Central Avenue, St. Petersburg; 727-897-9728
- Fresco's Ristorante, 300 2nd Avenue Northeast, St. Petersburg; 727-894-4429

Before & After the Game: Sports Bars

- Ferg's Sports Bar & Grill, 1320 Central Avenue, St. Petersburg; 727-822-4562
- Beef'O'Brady's, 226 37th Avenue North, St. Petersburg; 727-897-9686

Before & After the Game: Attractions

Note: Attractions listed in Chapters 13, 14, and 17 are also within striking distance. While you will find some overlap in the listings, you may want to check the other chapters before deciding what to do before and after the game here, especially if you are spending a few days in the area. For more possibilities, consult www.floridasbeach.com, the web site of the St. Petersburg / Clearwater Area Convention and Visitors Bureau.

- St. Petersburg Pier, on the waterfront at the end of Second Avenue Northeast; www.stpete-pier.com
  Come here to eat, shop, rent a bike, fish, hop a sightseeing cruise, or visit an aquarium. In addition to the pier, you'll find "The Pier," a five-story complex housing restaurants, shops, galleries, and an observation deck.
- Salvador Dali Museum, 1000 Third Street South, St. Petersburg; 727-823-3767, www.salvadordalimuseum.org
  Hours: Monday to Saturday 9:30 a.m. to 5:30 p.m. (Thursday to 8:00 p.m., Friday to 6:30 p.m.), Sunday noon to 5:30 p.m.
  Admission: Adults $15, Seniors (65+) $13.50, Students (10+) $10, Children (5 to 9) $4.
  The largest collection of Salvador Dali art outside of Spain. It takes a couple of hours to tour the permanent collection, which includes the bulk of Dali's most popular works.
- John's Pass Village & Boardwalk, 150 Boardwalk Place West, Madeira Beach; 727-394-0756, www.johnspass.com
  Billing itself as a "quaint turn-of-the-century fishing village," this large shopping, dining, and entertainment complex is also home to a large commercial and charter fishing fleet, as well as sightseeing cruise operators. Its boardwalk provides a scenic view of the waterfront.
- Great Explorations, The Children's Museum, 1925 4th Street North, St. Petersburg; 727-821-8992, www.greatexplorations.org
  Hours: Monday to Saturday 10:00 a.m. to 4:30 p.m., Sunday noon to 4:30 p.m., closed holidays
  Cost: General admission $9, Seniors $8
  Exhibits here invite kids to be active. Among the options: a climbing wall and a raceway where young visitors can build a tabletop race car from motor to axle and then race their vehicle on a slot car-type track.

- BayWalk Entertainment Center, 153 Second Avenue North, St. Petersburg; 727-895-9277; www.baywalkst-pete.com
  This 150,000 square foot shopping, dining, and entertainment complex in downtown St. Pete includes a 20-screen multiplex.
- Derby Lane, 10490 Gandy Boulevard North, St. Petersburg; 727-812-3339, www.derbylane.com
  Hours: Monday to Saturday, January to mid June. Gates open at 6:30 p.m., post at 7:30 p.m., and Monday, Wednesday, and Saturday gates open at 11:30 a.m., post at 12:30 p.m.
  Admission: $1
  Greyhounds race here nightly, except Sunday, during Spring Training season. General parking is free, or let the valet do it for $3. There's an all-you-can-eat buffet nightly (reservations suggested). If you tire of the dogs, you can play cards in the Poker Room till midnight.
  Note: You must be 12 or older to enter and 18 or older for admission to the card room.

Before & After the Game: Activities

- Fort Desoto Park, 3500 Pinellas Bayway, Tierra Verde; 727-582-2267, www.fortdesoto.com
  Hours: Open daily, hours for stores and rentals vary
  Admission: Free
  Located on Mullet Key, just south of St. Pete on SR 679 (Pinellas Bayway) at the entrance to Tampa Bay, Fort Desoto Park offers beaches, fishing, nature trails, kayaking, and even Paw Playground, a no-leash area where you can frolic with your dog.

Fishing

- Queen Fleet, 25 Causeway Boulevard, #52 and #53, Clearwater Beach; 727-446-7666
- Reef Tours, 3334 Crab Trap Lane, Hudson; 727-410-5551
- Charter Boat Two C's II, Slip 27 Municipal Marina, Clearwater Beach; 727-797-0784

Golf

- Airco Golf Course, 13690 Stonybrook Drive, Clearwater, 727-573-4653
- Bardmoor Golf Course, 8001 Cumberland Road, Largo; 727-392-1234
- Cypress Links at Mangrove Bay, 875 62nd Avenue Northeast, St. Petersburg; 727-551-3333
- Pasadena Yacht & Country Club, 6300 Pasadena Point Boulevard South, Gulfport; 727-381-7922
- Wentworth Golf Club, 2990 Wentworth Way, Tarpon Springs; 727-942-4760

Hotels Near the Ballpark

- Hampton Inn & Suites St. Petersburg/Downtown, 80 Beach Drive Northeast, St. Petersburg; 727-892-9900
- Heritage Holiday Inn Hotel, 234 Third Avenue North, St. Petersburg; 727-822-4814
- Hotel Ponce De Leon, 95 Central Avenue, St. Petersburg; 727-550-9300
- Pier Hotel, 253 Second Avenue North, St. Petersburg; 727-822-7500
- Randolph Hotel, 200 Fourth Street North, St. Petersburg; 727-822-4777
- Renaissance Vinoy Resort, 501 Fifth Avenue Northeast, St. Petersburg; 727-894-1000

Chapter 17

Toronto Blue Jays
Knology Park

Dunedin

Knology Park may not be the most breathtaking ballpark. It may be hard to find, and there's no question it looks a little run down. But whatever negatives the park has in terms of its aesthetics, it more than makes up for in its atmosphere and autograph possibilities. To sum it up, this is a fun park.

Finding it, however, is a chore. The stadium is located in the middle of a residential area with an elementary school over the outfield wall — not a place you would expect to see a Spring Training game. When you finally get there, you see an unimpressive, cement-covered stadium. At least it has flags, colored awnings, and other visuals to distract from the drab exterior.

You find the charm once you walk in, listen, and look around. You'll feel as if you have been transported to the Great White North of Canada. It seems as though everyone around you talks with a Canadian accent and ends their sentences with the proverbial "Eh?" This is the only Grapefruit League ballpark where more people know the words to "O Canada" than to "The Star Spangled Banner."

Unfortunately, the stadium has lost a little of its Canadian flair in the past few seasons. You'll find the Canadian staple, Labatts beer, at only two small carts now; Bud and Bud Light have replaced it as the beer of choice. Also, *The Globe & Mail*, Toronto's daily paper, is no longer advertised on the outfield wall. The program still caters to Canadians, however, with ads for phone rates to Canada and an equal exchange rate for

Photo courtesy of the Toronto Blue Jays.

tickets at Universal Studios. You'll also see an ad for the Tampa Bay Lightning, the area's hockey team. Now there are four Spring Training sites in the Tampa Bay area and every one of the others is located closer to the hockey arena than Knology Park, but the Lightning marketers know who loves hockey.

The Canadian atmosphere is just one of the factors that make Knology a fun place for baseball fans. Another is the autograph opportunities. You will get autographs here. You'll get as many as you want from both the home and visiting team — even if the visitors are the Yankees or the Braves.

This stadium is designed for autograph seekers. On the home (first base) side, the players walk along a four-foot chain link fence to get from the dugout to the clubhouse. The entrance to the clubhouse is adjacent to the end of the fans' area. A Blue Jays player must walk a great distance out of his way to avoid autograph hunters. On the visitors' side, the players have to walk through a passage that includes about 15 feet of fan access on one side. Visiting teams cannot even walk out of their way to avoid signing. They have no choice but to come close to the fans, and most players do not ignore requests for autographs when the fans are that close.

In fact, putting the fans close to the players is what Knology Park is all about. It is one of the more intimate parks in baseball, the second smallest in the Grapefruit League. Every seat is close to the action.

To top it off, tickets are available for most games and they are inexpensive, except for "premium" games.

While the town of Dunedin may be out of the way for many people, Knology Park is not to be missed. It's an experience you won't forget, eh?

Fast Facts

Knology Park at Grant Field
373 Douglas Avenue
Dunedin, FL 34698
727-733-0429
http://toronto.bluejays.mlb.com
http://www.dunedinbluejays.com/stadium/

Getting There

Take U.S. 19 to Sunset Point Road and go west 3.5 miles to Douglas Avenue. Turn right (north) onto Douglas and proceed to the stadium. It's one mile ahead on the right.

Note: Directions from Orlando, Tampa, Sarasota, and New Port Richie can be found on www.dunedinbluejays.com/stadium.

Parking

The stadium has several parking lots. One large lot is right next to the ballpark, and smaller lots are nearby. The latter are a bit of a walk from the park, but not a bad one as much of the way is paved.

Caution: The lots next to the park are reserved for handicapped parking ($10) and season ticket holders (don't ask). If you're eligible to park here, avoid the first few rows. It's like the splash zone at Shamu Stadium. Park in front and your car will get dinged. At least a dozen balls must have flown into the area during the game I attended and every one that hit a car caused damage.

One great place to park is the VFW lot across the street

from the stadium. It's not that much further than the stadium's parking and it's $8. Make sure you ask for a receipt because it counts as a charitable donation.

Otherwise, you can find parking nearby for anywhere from $5 to $10. If you poke around a bit and don't mind a short walk, you can probably park for free.

Cost: $5 to $10

Tickets

This is the Blue Jays. They aren't a big draw outside of the limited number of Canadians who make the trip to Florida or have migrated here. So even though Knology is the second smallest stadium in the Grapefruit League and one of the best places to watch Spring Training baseball, there are usually a couple of thousand tickets left for every game.

Of course, that does not include the games against marquee teams. Despite the fact that the Yankees play just 30 minutes away in Tampa's Legends Field, the Yankees vs. Blue Jays games have come within a few tickets of selling out, as have the Red Sox vs. Blue Jays games. So if you want to see the Yankees or Red Sox play here, you'll need to buy your tickets early.

You'll also pay more for these "premium" games, as reflected by the higher prices below. Premium prices might also be charged on other occasions, such as weekend games or games late in the season.

Capacity: 5,510

Average Attendance: 3,595

Ticket Prices:

Lower Club $18 / $24
Upper Club $15 / $20
Lower Outfield $15 / $20
Upper Outfield $13 / $17

For Tickets: 727-733-0429

Program

The Toronto Blue Jays' program ranks above average. While it could use more articles and a numerical roster of players, I give it high marks for its content. It has a seating chart, which is needed here. It has instructions on how to keep score,

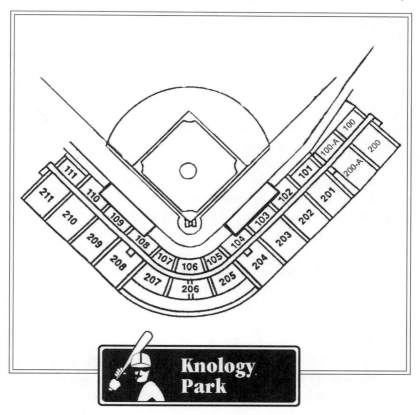

although they are not very detailed. It has mug shots of every player along with a brief biography and the player's previous-season and career stats. Perhaps the most impressive feature of the program I bought was a pullout brochure on the town of Dunedin. This quaint town has a lot to offer and the brochure had a list of every business establishment, along with a walking map of the route from the stadium to downtown — about a 15-minute stroll if you don't stop to shop, browse, or eat.

Everyone should know that Spring Training means economic development for the host town. Dunedin capitalizes on that better than any other community in the Grapefruit League. Unfortunately, this insert is not always included, but you may be able to pick one up at the park. Ask for it if you don't see it.

This program is a good buy.

Cost: $3

Seats

Thank goodness the program has a seating chart in it, because Knology Park has one of the more complicated ticket structures in baseball. Not that it's hard to find your seat; it's just that when you look at your ticket, you don't really know where to go. The lower club seats are just what they sound like. They are in the lower section of the stadium and run from near the outer end of one dugout to near the outer end of the other (sections 102 to 109). The upper club seats are the center three sections above the main seating aisle (205 to 207). The "Lower Outfield" seats are on the lower level and run from near the outer end of the dugouts to the ends of the stands (sections 102 to 100 and 110 to 111). These are great seats.

The "Upper Outfield" seats are the upper sections from the entrance-ways to the ends of the stadium on both sides (208 to 211 and 204 to 200). They, too, are close to the action.

Shade

A lack of shade is one of the few drawbacks to this stadium. The small roof doesn't provide much. If you want shade, make sure you sit on the first base side. As the afternoon progresses, the shade will creep down that side. Sit near the top if you want all shade and near the bottom for just a little shade. For all sun, sit on the third base side. There's plenty to be had.

Food & Drink

Go straight for the bratwurst. Do not pass Go.

One of the best things about this stadium is the smell of the barbecue. It's going full force on two big grills, one at the far end of the main concourse on the first base side and the other at an outdoor grill and café located next to the ticket building. Either place, you will be able to order some really good bratwurst, just like you'd find in the upper Midwest. (Take a pass on the hot dogs; they are just average.)

Souvenirs

You're not going to find much more than the typical stadium souvenirs here. There is just one small souvenir store. It's located underneath the first base grandstands and carries a basic selection of hats, t-shirts, golf shirts, and logoed baseballs and bats. If you want something unusual, browse the extensive memorabilia that one of the team's sponsors offers. You can't miss it; it's right outside the stadium store.

The best of both worlds: At Knology Park, fans turn out for a night game to soak up the atmosphere of this intimate ballpark without risking the fierce Florida sun.

Photos by Kelly Monaghan.

Autographs

If you are an autograph hound, this is the stadium for you. There is no better place to get signatures from your favorite players than at Knology Park.

To get signatures from the Toronto Blue Jays, you will want to walk from the main concourse to the end of the first base side. Look for the chain-link fence that separates the fan areas from the field. Hang out in the corner of that fence. The entrance to the Blue Jays clubhouse is right there. It's a swinging gate, no bigger than your fence at home. Every player must walk from that gate to the dugout. Most will stop and sign. In fact, the only way to avoid signing is by saying no, or by walking out to center field and then back again. A player has to really go way out of his way to avoid signing autographs.

It's even easier to get autographs from the visiting team. Go to the end of the third base side of the stadium. There are two prime spots. The first is at the end of the chain link fence. The players are forced to walk close to the fence to get to the visitors' clubhouse. Many will stop and sign. The second spot is hidden. Walk to your left (as you face the area the players have to walk around). You'll find a small tunnel with a door to the walkway. Go to that door. Some of the bigger stars will sign there.

A Game or an Experience?

The baseball is great here, but what makes this park so wonderful is the experience. You feel like you're visiting a foreign country. The Blue Jays have been training in Dunedin since their inception in 1977. You will meet and listen to people from Canada; you'll drink Canadian beer; you'll eat Canadian food. You can even sing along on the Canadian national anthem — the words are in the program. When you leave, you'll be an unofficial Canuck.

Adding to the atmosphere is a beer man with about the loudest voice anywhere in baseball. He keeps fans entertained and filled with beer.

Up Close & Personal?

This is the second smallest stadium in the Grapefruit League; you are going to be close to the players. No seat is more than 50 yards from the playing field. The one disappointment is that both bullpens are hidden from view, so you cannot see the pitchers warming up.

Getting Away

This stadium is hard to find and hard to leave. It is relatively easy to get out of the parking lots, especially because the crowds here tend to be small. Once you are out, however, you have to take a two-lane road through downtown Dunedin to get back to the main road.

Note: Check the date of Dunedin's annual March parade. On parade day, some streets are closed. If you're visiting that day, be prepared.

Before & After the Game: Restaurants

- Bon Appetit Restaurant, 150 Marina Plaza, Dunedin; 727-733-2151
- Casa Tina Gourmet Mexican & Vegetarian Cuisine, 369 Main Street, Dunedin; 727-734-9226
- Flanagan's Irish Pub, 465 Main Street, Dunedin; 727-736-4994
- Iris Family Restaurant, 234 Douglas Avenue, Dunedin; 727-734-0779
- Sea Sea Riders, 221 Main Street, Dunedin; 727-734-1445
- Bellini's, 487 Main Street, Dunedin; 727-733-5449

Before & After the Game: Sports Bars

- Crazy George's Sports Pub & Grill, 1425 Main Street, Dunedin; 727-736-1607
- Norton's Sports Bar & Grill, 1824 Main Street, Dunedin; 727-734-2053
- Eddie's Bar & Grill, 1283 Bayshore Boulevard, Dunedin; 727-734-2300

Before & After the Game: Attractions

Note: Attractions listed in Chapters 13, 14, and 16 are also within striking distance. While you will find some overlap in the listings, you may want to check the other chapters before deciding what to do before and after the game here, especially if you are spending a few days in the area. To find additional attractions in the Dunedin area, check www.floridasbeach.com, the web site of the St. Petersburg / Clearwater Area Convention and Visitors Bureau.

- Captain Memo's Original Pirate Cruise, 25 Causeway Boulevard, Dock 3, Clearwater Beach; 727-446-2587, www.captmemo.com
  Hours: Daily 10:00 a.m., 2:00 p.m., and sunset (6:00 p.m. in March)
  Cost: Adults $32 ($35 evening), Seniors (65+) $27, Juniors (13 to 17) $27, Children $22
  Explore the Gulf on this two-hour cruise from the Clearwater Marina. Champagne is served on the evening cruise.
- Celebration Station, 24546 U.S. Highway 19 North, Clearwater; 727-791-1799
  Hours: Sunday to Thursday noon to 9:00 p.m., Friday noon to midnight, Saturday 10:00 a.m. to midnight
  Cost: Varies
  This family oriented mini-theme park offers go-karts, bumper boats, games, miniature golf, batting cages, shows, and dining.

Before & After the Game: Activities

- Caladesi Island State Park, c/o Gulf Islands Geopark, #1 Causeway Boulevard, Dunedin; 727-469-5918 for park information, 727-734-5263 for ferry information
  Ferry service: Daily on the hour from 10:00 a.m., last return at 4:30 p.m.
  Fare (round trip): Adults $9, Children (4 to 12) $5.50 (no credit cards).
  Reached via a half hour ferry ride from Honeymoon Island, Caladesi Island boasts one of America's best

beaches — three miles of white sand — plus a three-mile nature trail, a kids' playground, shaded picnic areas, concessions, and changing facilities with showers. You can stay on Caladesi Island up to four hours. The ferry is at the west end of Dunedin Causeway, at the end of SR 586.

Note: Honeymoon Island is itself a state recreation area, with swimming, sunbathing, nature trails, bird observation areas, and concessions. It is open daily 8:00 a.m. to sundown.

- Moccasin Lake Nature Park, 2750 Park Trail Lane; Clearwater, 727-462-6024

Hours: Tuesday to Friday 9:00 a.m. to 5:00 p.m., Saturday and Sunday 10:00 a.m. to 6:00 p.m. Closed Monday unless it's a legal holiday.

Admission: Adults $3, Children (3 to 12) $2

Look and listen for nocturnal creatures on a special two-hour walk with a park guide. The park offers an environmental and energy education center along with a lake, upland forest, wetlands, and lots of native plant and animal species. A one-mile nature trail winds through the park. The Interpretive Center features wildlife exhibits, displays, and information.

Note: The park holds regular Night Hikes on the second Wednesday of every month. These start at 7:00 p.m. in March. The fee for these guided two-hour walks is $3.50 for adults and $2.50 for children ages 3 to 12.

Fishing

- Queen Fleet, 25 Causeway Boulevard, #52 and #53, Clearwater Beach; 727-446-7666
- Reef Tours, 3334 Crab Trap Lane, Hudson; 727-410-5551
- Charter Boat Two C's II, Slip 27, Municipal Marina, Clearwater Beach; 727-797-0784

Golf

- Airco Golf Course, 13690 Stonybrook Drive, Clearwater, 727-573-4653

- Bardmoor Golf Course, 8001 Cumberland Road, Largo; 727-392-1234
- Cypress Links at Mangrove Bay, 875 62nd Avenue Northeast, St. Petersburg; 727-551-3333
- Pasadena Yacht & Country Club, 6300 Pasadena Point Boulevard South, Gulfport; 727-381-7922
- Tumbleweeds, 424 Patricia Avenue, Dunedin; 727-736-3406
- Wentworth Golf Club, 2990 Wentworth Way, Tarpon Springs; 727-942-4760

Hotels Near the Ballpark

- Best Western Yacht Harbor Inn & Suites, 150 Marina Plaza, Dunedin; 727-733-4121
- Holiday Inn Express Hotel & Suites, 975 Broadway, Dunedin; 727-450-1200
- Meranova Guest Inn, 458 Virginia Lane, Dunedin; 727-733-9248

Chapter 18

Washington Nationals
Space Coast Stadium
Viera

It's been 12 years since Space Coast Stadium opened as the spring home of the Florida Marlins. Back then, the stadium was in the middle of a cow pasture, with almost nothing around it. Thankfully, the surrounding area has developed quite a bit since then, with new restaurants, shopping, and entertainment opening nearby.

However, three teams later, the inside of the park has changed little. It's even still decorated in the Marlins' teal and black, nowhere near the red and blue colors of the Washington Nationals, the stadium's current resident. While there are plans to redecorate, for now the place still feels like the Marlins' territory. This may, in part, be because the Marlins' minor league affiliate, the Brevard Manatees, still calls Space Coast Stadium home, and their mascot, who is decked out in teal and black, is very much in evidence.

In 2005, the Montreal Expos moved to Washington, D.C. and became the Washington Nationals. That year was a great year for Spring Training in Viera, a planned community between Melbourne and Cocoa. Space Coast Stadium saw an increase of 13,000 people from the year before. Seeing the Nationals was suddenly cool. There was a rush to find Nationals hats, shirts, and more.

But by 2006, the excitement about the Nationals cooled and attendance dropped to one of the lowest per-game averages in the state, with just 3,904 fans per game. That's less than half

Photo courtesy of Space Coast Stadium.

of the available seats at Space Coast Stadium, which is one of the largest stadiums in the Grapefruit League.

Yet even if the colors fit the team and the stands were full of Nationals' fans, the ballpark wouldn't come close to being the quintessential Spring Training stadium. Inside, it lacks any sort of architectural inspiration. It's mostly cement. The main walkway has a wide-open feel, but that's more from a lack of people than a lot of space. The stands are elevated, so the front row of seats is about six feet off the field of play. This creates a wall of separation between fans and players, while Spring Training is supposed to bring them together. And if you sit near the top of the stadium, you'll be quite a distance from the action.

The ballpark gets its name from its location on Florida's "Space Coast." It is just a few miles south of NASA's space shuttle launch pads at Kennedy Space Center. (You can see launches from the stadium if you are sitting in the berm section.) Somebody obviously thought it would be a great idea to tie into the "space" theme. The result is stadium signage with lettering that looks straight out of a 1960s' B-movie.

The classier side to this theme-ing are the flagpole memorials to the Columbia and Challenger space shuttle disasters. The area was greatly affected by both of these tragedies.

When you first get to the stadium, you will feel like you are in the middle of a cow pasture. In fact, it most likely was a cow pasture not long ago. In some parts of the parking lot, you need a four-wheel drive truck to get through the mud.

There's another hassle when you get your tickets. While the windows open at 11:00 a.m., as they do at other ballparks, the will-call window and the gates don't open until 11:30. This is later than at every other Spring Training park. However, there is a large practice field near the main entrance where the Nationals take turns at batting practice. If you arrive before the gates open, you can stand behind the outfield wall and pick up some extra baseballs while you wait.

In past years, the stadium only opened the berm on busy days, but the park now opens up the entire berm for all games. This is a nice place to watch a game, and it also provides a great opportunity to get autographs from the visiting team's catchers and pitchers, as the visitors' bullpen is cut into the berm.

While opening the berm was an improvement, the food at the stadium has declined since the Nationals took over. In the past, Space Coast Stadium had some of the best food in the Grapefruit League, but the day I went, the food was almost inedible. I got a turkey leg, took two bites, and threw it away. The chicken fingers were so-so and the fries were awful. In addition, I couldn't find the taco-in-a-helmet offering I'd loved on previous visits.

If you want visitors' autographs, this is an easy park to target. The visiting team must walk about 50 feet to get from the stadium to the bus. The area is open and roped off, giving fans an opportunity to meet the visitors. Getting Nationals' autographs is a bit tougher, but it can be done, especially if you come when the gates open at 11:30 a.m.

Overall, it is easy to get tickets here. Just don't come expecting a traditional Spring Training experience.

Fast Facts

Space Coast Stadium
5800 Stadium Parkway
Melbourne, FL 32940
321-633-4487
http://washington.nationals.mlb.com

Getting There

Take I-95 to Exit 195, Fiske Boulevard South. Follow Fiske south. It will turn into Stadium Parkway, which will take you directly to the ballpark.

Parking

Space Coast Stadium has some of the worst parking in the Grapefruit League. It's not well marked and it's a distance from the stadium. The lots are glorified cow pastures. Watch out for the mud and anthills.

Note: There is a parking lot next to the stadium. It is reserved for employees and handicapped parking. However, it does not say that anywhere. You won't find out until you drive in and get turned away.

Cost: $5

Tickets

This is the easiest ticket to get in all of Spring Training. The Nationals lack a large fan base because they only recently started playing in Washington, and the stadium, situated between Melbourne and Cocoa, is far from any large metropolis. (Orlando is about an hour and a half away.) It averages 45 percent empty, meaning there are thousands of tickets available on most game days. Of course, you have to plan ahead if a marquee visitor is scheduled.

Although general admission is just $9 and berm seating only $7, the top-price seat is more expensive than the average for the League.

Capacity: 8,100

Average Attendance: 3,904

Ticket Prices:
> Batter's Box $20
> Box Seats $16
> Reserved Seats $13
> Bleachers $9
> Berm seats (available only on game day) $7

For Tickets: 321-633-4487

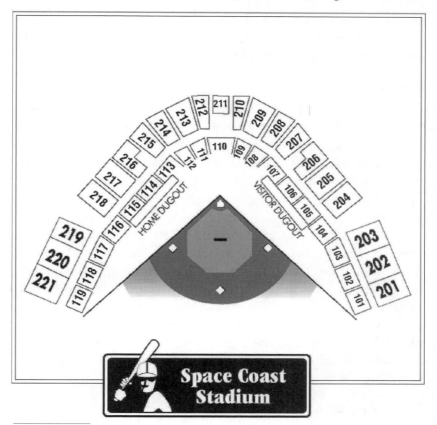

Program

There isn't a program to be found. Instead, there is a score-card with a paper insert listing the day's line-up. The scorecard is the same for the Nationals and the minor league team. If you don't keep score, don't bother.

Cost: $2

Seats

It's easy to find seats in the reserved sections. As in most stadiums, the Reserved seats are above the main seating aisle and Box seats below. To get to the berm, cross a bridge from the end of the left field line. It's easy to find.

Shade

Wear sunscreen. This park is oriented in the wrong direction. If you sit on the visitors' (third base) side, there is no shade during the game and you will be facing the sun for most of it. On the first base side, the small roof provides a little shade, but not until near the end of the game.

Food & Drink

One of the great things about Space Coast Stadium used to be the food. But unfortunately, in 2006, the food was about the worst tasting stadium food I've ever had in my life.

Let's start with the decision to remove one of my favorite items, the Taco in the Helmet. This was a unique dish, only found in this park, but in 2006, the taco in the helmet was no more.

When I walked the park and didn't find my favorite food, I went looking for my second-favorite, the turkey leg. In years past, the turkey leg came straight off the grill, and was fantastic. This year, it was sitting in a warmer, wrapped in foil, apparently pre-cooked. The turkey was soggy and flavorless. I threw it away and went for the chicken fingers, which were bland, but edible. The fries, however, were horrible. Even my son, who would eat chicken fingers for every meal if he had the choice, agreed with my assessment.

Souvenirs

There are plenty of opportunities to purchase souvenirs at Space Coast Stadium, starting with when you pick up your tickets. There is a small store next to the ticket window. It offers plenty of choice, with many different types of merchandise. (It is strange to go into the store looking for Nationals' merchandise and see so much teal and black from the Marlins' minor league affiliate, the Brevard Manatees, however.)

Once you are in the stadium, you will find a small souvenir stand near the entrance. This carries a limited selection, but unlike the store outside, it is more focused on the Major League teams than the minor leagues.

Autographs

It's easier to get autographs from visitors than from Nationals. Simply leave the game a couple of innings early and walk to the right of the entrance bridge. You will see a roped-off sidewalk that leads to a bus. All of the visiting team will walk along the rope line. The first players out will usually stop and sign. The slow pokes will rush past you so as not to hold up the bus.

If you want Nationals' autographs, get to the game when the gates open at 11:30 a.m. and position yourself to catch some of the players as they walk from the practice field to the stadium. They have to walk about the length of a football field, giving you plenty of opportunity. Of course, you are at their mercy. Some run quickly past, while others sign as they walk.

Once inside the stadium, there aren't many opportunities. The best place to try is a section next to the first base dugout that was originally built for news photographers. It is down a few stairs, making it the only place in the stadium where you are on the same level as the playing field. Some of the players will come over to sign if you call to them.

Note: This area closes about 20 minutes before gametime, again right as one of the prime autograph times starts.

A Game or an Experience?

You're here to watch a game. Yes, there are some garden-variety contests between innings, but just the typical contests you'll find at most ballparks. Also, the combo of the new Nationals team and a relatively new park work against this being an experience.

Up Close & Personal?

You're going to feel like you are in a Major League Baseball stadium here. The main problem is the height of the stands. The front row is about six feet off the playing field, separating fans from players. The stadium's large size compounds the problem. If you buy a ticket for a seat near the top of the stadium, you are going to be quite a ways from the field.

Getting Away

There is a two-lane road running by the stadium that connects with the main roads. Fortunately, there are not a lot of cars in the parking lot, and thus not a lot of traffic leaving the game.

If you are heading for I-95, make sure you go north. While going south will get you home, the northern route is much quicker.

Before & After the Game: Restaurants

- Durango Steakhouse, 6765 North Wickham Road, Melbourne; 321-259-2955
- Charlie & Jake's Bar-B-Que, 6300 North Wickham Road, Suite 137, Melbourne; 321-752-7675
- Rendezvous Restaurant, Imperial's Hotel, 8298 North Wickham Road, Melbourne; 321-255-0077
- Cracker Barrel Old Country Store, 7225 George T. Edwards Drive, Melbourne; 321-242-0350

Before & After the Game: Sports Bars

- Mulligan's Grille, 2300 Club House Drive, Viera; 321-639-3487
- Beef 'O'Brady's, 1450 North Courtenay Parkway, Merritt Island; 321-455-6665
- Chalkies Billiards & Sports Bar, 925 North Courtenay Parkway, Merritt Island; 321-449-0189

Before & After the Game: Attractions

Visit www.space-coast.com, the web site of Florida's Space Coast Office of Tourism for additional possibilities.

- Brevard Zoo, 8225 North Wickham Road, Melbourne; 321-254-9453, www.brevardzoo.org
  Hours: Daily except Thanksgiving and Christmas 9:30 a.m. to 5:00 p.m.
  Admission: Adults $10, Seniors (60+) $9, Children (2 to 12) $7
  Over 550 animals including alligators, giant anteaters, bobcats, river otters, eagles, and several primate species are among the inhabitants here. Kids can feed the parrots and explore the "Paws-On Interactive Zone."
- Sterling Casino Lines, 180 Christopher Columbus Drive — Terminal 2, Port Canaveral; 800-765-5711, 321-784-8558, www.sterlingcasinolines.com

Hours: Sails twice daily at 11:00 a.m. and 7:00 p.m.
Admission: Free

Features four casinos, five cocktail lounges, a nightclub, and an outdoor reggae deck. Cruises last five hours. You must be 21 to sail. Reservations required.

- Kennedy Space Center Visitors Center, Merritt Island (due east of Cocoa); 321-449-4444, www.kennedyspacecenter.com

Hours: Daily, except Christmas and mission launch days, 9:00 a.m. to 5:30 p.m. (last tour to Apollo/Saturn V Center leaves at 2:15 p.m.)

Admission: Adults $31*, Children (3 to 11) $21*

Visit the home of the country's space exploration program. Among the highlights of this attraction are exhibits (traditional and interactive) on all aspects of America's space program, IMAX movies, a live astronaut encounter, and a visit to the Apollo/Saturn V Center. There you will see an actual Saturn V moon rocket and experience a re-creation of man's first landing on the moon.

*Add $7 to include admission to the Astronaut Hall of Fame, just west of KSC on State Route 405, which houses astronaut memorabilia and interactive activities that simulate the experience of being in space.

- Andretti Thrill Park, 3960 South Babcock Street, Melbourne; 321-956-6706, www.andrettithrillpark.com

Hours: Monday to Thursday 11:00 a.m. to 10:00 p.m., Friday and Saturday 10:00 a.m. to 1:00 a.m., Sunday noon to 10:00 p.m.

Cost: Varies by ride, with most $3 to $6

The park lives up to its name with go-kart tracks, bumper boats, an 18-hole minors pro-golf course, laser tag, an arcade room, and three kiddie rides.

- Super Flea & Farmers Market, 4835 West Eau Gallie Boulevard, Melbourne; 321-242-9124

Hours: Friday, Saturday, Sunday 9:00 a.m. to 4:00 p.m.

Admission: Free

Before & After the Game: Activities

Eco-Tours

- Grasshopper Airboat Ecotours, on the St. Johns River west of Cocoa; 321-631-2990, www.airboatecotours.com
  Hours: Flexible
  Cost: Adults $35, Children (7 to 12) $25 (appropriate for kids 7 and older)
  Look for alligators, eagles, and other wildlife on these 90-minute tours of the marshes of the St. Johns River. Reservations required.
- Island Boat Lines Water Taxi & Eco-Boat Tours, Space Coast Waterways, Merritt Island; 321-454-7414, www.islandboatlines.com
  Hours: Monday to Saturday 10:00 a.m., 1:00 p.m., and sunset, Sunday 12:00 p.m., 3:00 p.m., and sunset
  Cost: Varies by tour (for example, Adults $25, Seniors and Children $23 for a 2-hour cruise)
  See manatees, birds, and dolphin as you explore coastal estuaries in a 55-passenger boat. Reservations required. (321-302-0544).

Deep-Sea Fishing

- Miss Cape Canaveral, 670 Glen Cheek Drive, Cape Canaveral; 321-783-5274
- Obsession Fishing Charters, Sunrise Marina, Cape Canaveral; 321-453-3474
- Orlando Princess Deep Sea Fishing, 650 Glen Cheek Drive, Port Canaveral; 321-784-6300

Golf

- Viera East Golf Club, 2300 Clubhouse Drive, Viera; 321-639-6500
- Aquarina Country Club, 7500 South Highway A1A, Melbourne Beach; 321-728-0600
- Baytree National Golf Links, 8207 National Drive, Melbourne; 321-259-9060
- Harbor City Municipal Golf Course, 2750 Lake Wash-

ington Road, Melbourne; 321-255-4606
- Indian River Colony Club, 1936 Freedom Drive, Melbourne; 321-255-6050, extension 224 (pro shop)

Hotels Near the Ballpark

- America's Best Value Inn, 4500 West New Haven Avenue, Melbourne; 321-724-2051
- La Quinta Inn and Suites, 7200 George T. Edwards Drive, Melbourne; 321-242-9400
- Hampton Inn – Melbourne, 194 Dike Road, Melbourne; 321-956-6200
- Imperial's Hotel & Conference Center, 8298 North Wickham Road, Melbourne; 321-255-0077
- The Swiss Inn & Tennis Center, 3220 South Fiske Boulevard, Rockledge; 321-631-9445

Photo by Kelly Monaghan.

Tradition is a big part of the Spring Training experience. Here players and fans alike stand to pay their respects to the flag during the playing of the National Anthem at Legends Field in Tampa.

Chapter 19

The Rankings

How The Stadiums Stack Up

Here are my purely subjective rankings of seventeen Florida Spring Training sites, based on my 2006 visits.

Each stadium is ranked on five factors:

- *Intimacy:* How close do you feel to the players and the action?

- *Autographs:* How easy is it to get them?

- *Comfort:* How comfortable is it in terms of the seats, the balance of sun and shade, and getting to and from the parking lot?

- *Food:* How tasty is the food? Do you have lots of options? Are the concession stands easy to locate and the lines manageable?

- *Style:* How attractive is the park overall? Do the design elements fit the site and the team?

I rank each factor on a 1 to 10 scale, with 10 the highest. The scores on each factor are then added to arrive at a final score for the stadium. A perfect score would be 50.

Breaking Ties

When there is a tie in the numerical score, the stadium with the higher ratings for Intimacy and Autographs is ranked higher because these are the essence of Spring Training and the factors that most separate the Spring Training experience from a trip to a major league ballpark.

1. Holman Stadium - Vero Beach
Los Angeles Dodgers (Chapter 10)

Holman Stadium in Dodgertown is Spring Training the way it is supposed to be. It's quaint, old, and intimate. No other Spring Training site lets you get closer to the players. Holman also offers "Dodger Dogs," the staple nourishment for Dodgers watchers.

Intimacy:	10
Autographs:	10
Comfort:	8
Food:	8
Style:	10
Total:	**46**

2. Osceola County Stadium - Kissimmee
Houston Astros (Chapter 9)

Osceola is the smallest stadium in the Grapefruit League, and that's a good thing. You feel you are really part of the game here, regardless of where you are sitting, and you will have ample autograph opportunities. The park also gets extra credit for its attention to children.

Intimacy:	10
Autographs:	9
Comfort:	9
Food:	7
Style:	9
Total:	**44**

3. Bright House Networks Field - Clearwater
Philadelphia Phillies (Chapter 14)

The park is a perfect blend of the new and the old. There are great places for fan interaction, it's a beautiful stadium, and the food is outstanding. The bar area in right field certainly helps to move this park to almost the top of the list.

Intimacy:	8
Autographs:	8
Comfort:	9
Food:	9
Style:	10
Total:	**44**

4. Knology Park - Dunedin Toronto Blue Jays (Chapter 17)

Dunedin offers the best autograph opportunities in the Grapefruit League. There are few places where players can hide from fans. People actually know the words to the Canadian national anthem here, and it's a plus that Labatt is the main beer served.

Intimacy:	9
Autographs:	10
Comfort:	8
Food:	7
Style:	6
Total:	**40**

5. Roger Dean Stadium - Jupiter Florida Marlins, St. Louis Cardinals (Chapter 8)

This is a small stadium with fairly decent access to the players, comfortable stands, and wide and airy concourses. But there aren't enough opportunities for autographs and the lack of a roof is a minus.

Intimacy:	9
Autographs:	6
Comfort:	8
Food:	9
Style:	8
Total:	**40**

6. Tradition Field - Port St. Lucie
New York Mets (Chapter 12)

One of the best berms in baseball, picnic tables, and seats close to the field improve this stadium incredibly over last year. Plus, it looks a whole lot better when you're walking up to it. Of course, spending $10 million on anything should improve it significantly.

Intimacy:	7
Autographs:	7
Comfort:	8
Food:	9
Style:	8
Total:	**39**

7. McKechnie Field - Bradenton
Pittsburgh Pirates (Chapter 15)

The tickets are cheap, fans run the ballpark, and it's a beautiful stadium. This is perhaps the most picturesque park in the Grapefruit League. It's easy to get autographs and there's great food to be had. If it weren't for the uncomfortable chairs and obstructed views, McKechnie Field would rank number 2.

Intimacy:	10
Autographs:	8
Comfort:	4
Food:	6
Style:	10
Total:	**38**

8. City of Palms Park - Fort Myers
Boston Red Sox (Chapter 4)

Outside, City of Palms is gorgeous. Inside, it's pretty but has some glitches: food choices are limited and the souvenir shop's crowded. There's also too much shade for me. One plus is, you'll find a great spot to watch the players when they're not on the field.

Intimacy: 7
Autographs: 7
Comfort: 9
Food: 6
Style: 8
Total: **37**

---

9. The Ballpark at Disney's Wide World of Sports® Complex - Lake Buena Vista
Atlanta Braves (Chapter 2)

This is certainly one of the prettiest parks in the League, and one of the more entertaining, but it is designed for the casual baseball fan. People who want to get close to the players and experience traditional Spring Training should look elsewhere. Those who just want to go to a ball game will likely find it perfect.

Intimacy: 4
Autographs: 3
Comfort: 9
Food: 9
Style: 9
Total: **34**

---

10. Fort Lauderdale Stadium - Fort Lauderdale
Baltimore Orioles (Chapter 3)

It's starting to show its age, but Fort Lauderdale Stadium has the most comfortable box seats in sports. The outfield wall covered in plants is a nice touch. However, the concessions are limited and you can't walk from the grandstands to the bleachers.

Intimacy: 8
Autographs: 6
Comfort: 8
Food: 4
Style: 6
Total: **32**

11. Bill Hammond Stadium - Fort Myers
Minnesota Twins (Chapter 11)

There's a real dichotomy here. The outside is absolutely beautiful, but inside is just average. The park has fairly good concession offerings and the bar hidden under the stands is a neat touch. Also, stadium management understands how to keep fans entertained.

Intimacy:	5
Autographs:	5
Comfort:	6
Food:	8
Style:	8
Total:	**32**

12. Joker Marchant Stadium - Lakeland
Detroit Tigers (Chapter 7)

This stadium would rank higher if it weren't for the big net along the first base line that separates fans from the field. There are some elements here that don't fit, like the large bleachers, but overall Joker Marchant is a quaint park, with a great berm.

Intimacy:	6
Autographs:	3
Comfort:	7
Food:	7
Style:	9
Total:	**32**

13. Chain of Lakes Park - Winter Haven
Cleveland Indians (Chapter 6)

There are only so many coats of paint that'll keep a stadium looking new before it becomes a lost cause This ballpark is starting to show its age. Unfortunately, stadium expansions have taken away most of the autograph opportunities that once made up for its other failings.

Intimacy:	8
Autographs:	3
Comfort:	6
Food:	4
Style:	9
Total:	**30**

14. Ed Smith Stadium - Sarasota Cincinnati Reds (Chapter 5)

Unfortunately, this nondescript ballpark has a critical design flaw. The placement of the clubhouse door away from the bleachers allows players to avoid autograph seekers altogether. If it weren't for the great concessions, Ed Smith Stadium would rank even lower than it does.

Intimacy:	7
Autographs:	2
Comfort:	6
Food:	9
Style:	5
Total:	**29**

15. Legends Field - Tampa New York Yankees (Chapter 13)

You'll find some of the best food in the entire Grapefruit League here, but the stadium itself is the antithesis of Spring Training as fans like it. It is big, but good seats for real fans are limited because so many are sold to no-show corporate ticket holders. The police presence is overbearing and access to the players is severely limited.

Intimacy:	1
Autographs:	3
Comfort:	7
Food:	10
Style:	7
Total:	**28**

16. Space Coast Stadium - Melbourne
Washington Nationals (Chapter 18)

The teal and black décor here is out of step with the Nationals' red, white, and blue colors. The stadium is in the middle of nowhere and easily missed.

Intimacy:	5
Autographs:	4
Comfort:	7
Food:	2
Style:	4
Total:	**22**

17. Progress Energy Park - St. Petersburg
Tampa Bay Devil Rays (Chapter 16)

While the autograph opportunities and the sea gulls make for an interesting day in the ballpark, the stadium itself is best regarded as an oven. You will get sunburned in this cement enclosure even if you lather on the sun block.

Intimacy:	4
Autographs:	7
Comfort:	4
Food:	2
Style:	4
Total:	**21**

Chapter 20

Five Great
Spring Training Trips

Themed, Week-Long Touring Plans
to the Best of Baseball in Florida

Perhaps the greatest thing about planning a Spring Training vacation is that no matter what part of central or southern Florida you want to visit, you will find several ballparks within an hour's drive of each other. It's quite easy to pick a central location and spend a week just going to baseball games. But while true fans might like nothing better than spending an entire vacation watching baseball, eating hot dogs, and soaking up rays, they would cheat themselves of much that Florida has to offer.

Going to Florida's Central Gulf Coast (St. Pete to Fort Myers) without taking time to visit its wonderful Gulf of Mexico beaches, for instance, or visiting the Orlando area without experiencing any of its world-class attractions, would be just plain perverse. And chances are, your significant others wouldn't stand for it anyway.

Here then are five perfect week-long trips that center around baseball but allow time to sample other attractions and activities. Each itinerary assumes that you will be driving from park to park, and each is themed. Since several ballparks fit into more than one theme, you'll find some overlap from trip to trip. The longest drive between ballparks in any given itinerary is less than a day, and many are within an hour's drive of each other. If you're a die-hard fan, you may want to combine two itineraries and spend two weeks basking in the joys of Spring Training.

Caution: Itineraries cannot always be followed exactly as suggested because team schedules won't always cooperate. Make sure you check the game schedules for the teams and stadiums you plan to visit as soon as they are announced (generally in mid December). The best way to do this is to visit the team web sites listed in the Stadium chapters.

Then adjust your start date and itinerary as needed to fit the playing schedules. Some itineraries are more flexible than others. I'll make more specific comments and suggestions in each of the itineraries below.

A quick overview of the five itineraries follows. To give yourself enough time to enjoy all of the activities in each itinerary, plan on arriving in the morning of Day One and leaving in the evening of Day Seven.

Note: If you have time to spend an extra day, you'll find suggestions for an optional leisure day in Itinerary Two.

1. ***Tampa-St. Petersburg.*** Visit five ballparks, including two of the top five in my rankings, plus some of Florida's best attractions — all without changing hotels.

2. ***Spring Training History.*** Visit ballparks old and new in the five communities with the longest histories of hosting the same team and get a taste of small town and rural Florida as you drive from the east coast to the west.

3. ***Baseball and Boardwalks.*** Visit three central Florida ballparks and combine theme park thrills with America's favorite pastime.

4. ***The Gulf Coast.*** Visit five ballparks, including the home stadiums of two of the Grapefruit League's top teams, in this trip along Florida's scenic Gulf Coast.

5. ***The East Coast.*** Visit the "shrine of Spring Training" and three other ballparks and get a feel for Florida's small coastal towns and two of its largest cities.

Note: You'll find more information, including addresses and phone numbers, for the restaurants and attractions mentioned in these itineraries in the Stadium chapters.

Itinerary One:
Tampa - St. Petersburg

This trip may offer the best combination of experiences available to fans of Spring Training. You'll visit five ballparks and experience the essence of both traditional Spring Training and its newer variations. You'll enjoy two of the top five Spring Training parks as well as two of the three I put at the bottom. You'll see one of the hottest teams in baseball along with a couple that few people follow. In addition, you'll get to experience some of Florida's top attractions. And here's the best part: you won't have to change hotels even once. All of the attractions and ballparks are within an hour's drive of a central location.

Flexibility: Switching days to match the ballparks' game schedules is easy in this itinerary because you stay in the same hotel all week.

Note: You can fly in and out of either Tampa International Airport or St. Petersburg/Clearwater International Airport.

Day One: At Leisure

Arrive. Pick up your rental car, take I-275 to the St. Petersburg / Clearwater International Airport exit, 31B, and check into your hotel. When I made this trip, I tried both the Comfort Inn (3580 Ulmerton Road, Clearwater; 727-573-1171) and the Courtyard by Marriott (3131 Executive Drive, Clearwater; 727-572-8484) at this exit. Both were suitable, clean, and affordable. They were also the perfect launching point for the itinerary.

You're probably tired, so take it easy today. If you arrive early, head west from the hotel and spend the day at the beach. If you arrive later in the day, spend the afternoon or evening at the St. Petersburg Pier. It's a beauty — with shops, restaurants, and a small aquarium. You can pay to feed the pelicans. Or rent fishing poles and try your luck in the waters of Tampa Bay. Whatever you do, get home early because you have a big day ahead of you.

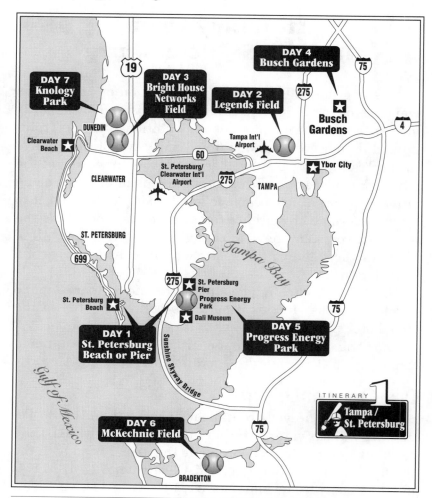

Day Two: Legends Field / Yankees
(see Chapter 13)

Sleep in a little and enjoy breakfast at the Perkins near the hotel, but make sure you leave enough time for traffic. Tampa is one of the most congested cities in Florida. If this is a workday, you're going to get into a traffic jam. Allow about 30 minutes to get from the hotel to the ballpark.

Plan on arriving at Legends Field around 10:30 a.m. to watch the Yankees on the practice field and claim a spot to get an autograph; it's no easy task here. After practice is over, enter the stadium, watch the game, and enjoy the food. The game will end around 5:00 p.m.

You should be hungry again by this time. Stop at one of the restaurants along Dale Mabry. If you want something really fancy, go to Bern's Steakhouse. It will cost you a couple hundred dollars for two people with drinks and dessert, but the steaks are fantastic. Non-meat eaters and the more adventuresome may prefer Bern's sister restaurant, Sidebern's.

Instead of heading back to the hotel after dinner, plan on some evening entertainment. Go east on I-275 to I-4, then east (towards Orlando) on I-4. You can go to Ybor City, where there is a Sega GameWorks, a large movie complex, and plenty of clubs, or you can keep on going to the Seminole Casino Tampa. They have bingo, slots, and low-stakes poker. Either one is a fun option.

Day Three: Bright House Networks Field / Phillies
(see Chapter 14)

Wake up early and grab a quick bite to eat. You're going to experience the best in beaches and baseball today. Drive straight west to U.S. 19 North, take a right and go to Gulf-to-Bay Boulevard (SR 60). Take a left onto the boulevard. This will lead you to Clearwater Beach, where you can enjoy a couple of hours in the sun.

Around 11:00 a.m. pack up your beach bag and sunscreen and head back to Clearwater for a Philadelphia Phillies game. Enjoy the game. When it's over, head back to the beach, making sure you get there before 6:00 p.m. That's when the sun goes down, and there's nothing quite like a sunset on the Gulf of Mexico as the sun slowly sinks below the flat waters. After the colors fade, head back to your hotel and get a good night's sleep.

Day Four: Busch Gardens Africa
(see Chapter 13 "Attractions")

Take a break from baseball today. A trip to Tampa Bay is incomplete without a visit to Busch Gardens. You can sleep in a little, but not too late. The park generally opens at 10:00 a.m. and you'll want to get there around opening time to experience all it has to offer. Allow about 45 minutes for the drive from the hotel. The park is a couple of miles off I-275 on Busch Boulevard.

Enjoy the day riding roller coasters, visiting exotic animals, and watching live shows. You'll be tired when you leave, so go straight to the hotel after dinner and head right to bed.

Day Five: Progress Energy Park / Devil Rays
(see Chapter 16)

Today is focused on baseball and the arts. Wake up early and drive to downtown St. Petersburg. On Fourth Avenue is the largest collection of Salvador Dali art outside of Spain. It takes a couple of hours to tour the permanent collection, which includes the bulk of Dali's most popular works.

Once you've had your fill of melting clocks and a hologram called "Alice Cooper's Brain," head north on Fourth Avenue to Progress Energy Park, year-round home of the Tampa Bay Devil Rays. While it's not the greatest venue, it's still baseball and you'll get to see a ballpark that has been around for a while.

Enjoy the game and when it's over, take a walk around downtown St. Petersburg if you haven't already done so. The St. Petersburg Pier is a great attraction. Eat dinner on the top floor of "The Pier" for a great view of Tampa and St. Petersburg.

Day Six: McKechnie Field / Pirates
(see Chapter 15)

Today, you're going to try your hand at fishing and baseball. Leave your hotel room around 7:30 or 8:00 in the morning and travel south on I-275. After you cross the beautiful Skyway Bridge, you will see a sign for the south fishing pier. Take the turn, pay the fee (there is a small charge to get onto the pier), and proceed the four miles to the end of the pier. Stop at the bait shop. There you can pick up a couple dozen shrimp and some fishing poles. You'll have fun catching Spanish mackerel, bluefish, and sometimes even bigger species. You can catch and release a dozen in a couple of hours if you're lucky.

Leave the pier around 10:30 a.m. and head to one of the best ballparks in Spring Training, McKechnie Field in Bradenton. This one is a real treat. If you want a great snack or an after-game meal, stop off in the restaurant next door to the park.

Go to bed early and get a good night's sleep so that you can get an early start tomorrow.

Day Seven: Knology Park / Blue Jays
(see Chapter 17)

Today is your last pitch of the trip. Hopefully, you've booked a night flight out, because you don't want to miss a visit to one of the best baseball experiences in Spring Training, Knology Park in Dunedin, Spring Training home of the Toronto Blue Jays.

If you get up early, you can drive to downtown Dunedin for breakfast at one of the town's quaint restaurants. Afterward, you can shop and walk around this great downtown area. But don't get too wrapped up in it. You'll want to get to the game early to get autographs. This is the best park in the league for autograph seekers. Then enjoy the game, eat a bratwurst or two, and sip a cold Labatt beer.

Afterward, it's off to the airport, concluding your week of baseball in Tampa Bay.

Itinerary Two:
Spring Training History

While this trip involves more driving than any of the other four itineraries, it may be the most rewarding. You'll be visiting the five towns with the longest histories of hosting the same team. You'll visit the shrine of Spring Training, Dodgertown, along with the newest stadium in the League in Clearwater. You'll get a taste of Canada and a taste of small town Florida. If you have the time, you can add a day to explore the Gulf Coast and make this an eight-day trip (see below).

Flexibility: It is essential to check the game schedules for these five ballparks well in advance — say in late December or early January — so that you can time your visit for a seven-day stretch when the itinerary will work as laid out. The only days you can easily switch are five and six, because this itinerary takes you on a long loop across the state and does not allow time for doubling back and forth. You start and end at Orlando International Airport.

Tip: Get a rental car with unlimited mileage.

Day One: At Leisure

Arrive at Orlando International Airport, rent your car, and take the Beeline Expressway (SR 528) east to I-95. Take I-95 south to Vero Beach. It's about an hour and a half drive from the airport.

Note: The Beeline Expressway is a toll road, so be prepared to ante up. It's the fastest and only convenient route from the airport to I-95.

Stay at one of the hotels on the beach and enjoy the sand and water. A fantastic option is Disney's Vero Beach Resort (9250 Island Grove Terrace, U.S. A1A, Vero Beach; 772-234-2000). It's a time-share but it accepts overnight guests. (Best to book ahead, of course). Wrap up the day with a leisurely evening stroll down the beach, which has yet to be spoiled by the development found in most other Florida coastal communities. But don't stay up too late; tomorrow will be busy.

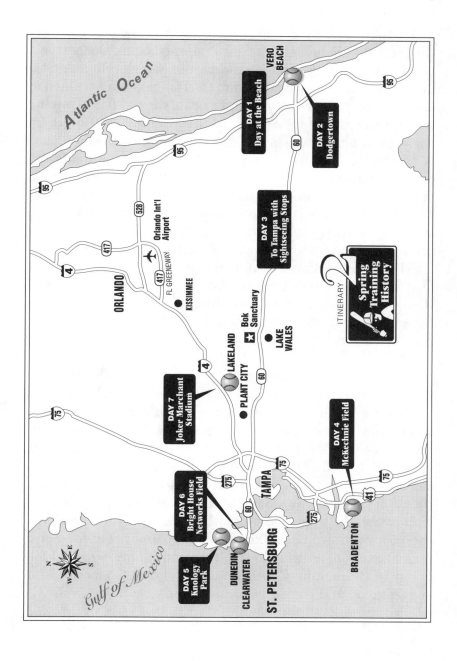

Day Two: Dodgertown / Dodgers
(see Chapter 10)

It's time to visit the shrine of Spring Training, Dodgertown, the place where modern Spring Training began. Dodgertown is the oldest Spring Training complex in Florida. Holman Stadium was built there in 1953 and the Dodgers have trained in it ever since. You'll want to spend most of the day here, walking the practice fields and taking in the atmosphere. So get up early, get a bite to eat, and plan to arrive around 9:30 a.m.

Spend the morning walking around the practice fields and observing the players. Then, between 11:00 and noon, position yourself near the stadium so that you can catch the players as they walk to the stadium from the practice fields. If you're standing nearby, you'll have great opportunities to get autographs and to talk to some of baseball's great players.

The game itself starts at 1:00 p.m. Get yourself a Dodger Dog from the concession stand before you head for your seat. It's one of baseball's great treats. After the game, get the fixings for a picnic and eat it on the beach. Enjoy the evening.

Day Three: Driving and Sightseeing

Today is mainly a driving day. You're going to take SR 60 all the way across the state from Vero Beach to Tampa. On the way, you'll get a look at small-town and rural Florida and have the chance to visit such places as Historic Bok Sanctuary in Lake Wales (see Chapter 6 or 7), just a few miles north of route 60. (Take SR 17 / Alt. U.S. 27 north to Burns Avenue and follow the signs.) This old time attraction fits in perfectly with the theme of this itinerary. You may also want to stop at roadside fruit stands for some great strawberries. Or if you prefer, you can pick your own near Plant City. Keep an eye out for signs.

At Brandon, east of Tampa, turn south onto I-75 and follow it to Bradenton. Check into a hotel (see Chapter 15 for suggestions) and have a leisurely night.

Day Four: McKechnie Field / Pirates
(see Chapter 15)

Today, you're going to visit one of the top parks in Spring

Training, McKechnie Field. Treat yourself to a leisurely breakfast; then pack up, check out, and head for the ballpark. The Pittsburgh Pirates have been training in Bradenton since 1969. Although the stadium has been renovated, it has a classic look that few in the Grapefruit League can match. Enjoy the atmosphere, the intimacy, and the autographing opportunities.

There's not a lot to do in Bradenton, so after the game, head for Clearwater Beach. Go north on U.S. 41 to U.S. 19 and I-275. When U.S. 19 and I-275 split, stay on 19 until you reach SR 60 (Gulf-to-Bay Boulevard).

Then turn west (left) toward the beach. Check into a nice hotel on the beach (see Chapter 14) and enjoy the night breezes. Relax. You'll be staying here two nights.

Day Five: Knology Park / Blue Jays
(see Chapter 17)

Today, you'll go to Canada. But first, have a leisurely morning. Eat an early breakfast at a café overlooking the ocean. Then spend the early morning hours collecting seashells on the beach or relaxing with a good book.

About 10:30, head to Dunedin to see the Toronto Blue Jays. The Blue Jays have been training in this small Clearwater suburb for over a quarter century. Make sure you get to the park early so that you can get some autographs. During the game, enjoy the Labatt Beer and the bratwurst. This is the only park that serves them both.

After the game, stroll down the street to downtown Dunedin. It's just a few blocks away from the park. You'll find quaint shops and great restaurants. When you're ready to call it a day, head back to your hotel.

Day Six: Bright House Networks Field / Phillies
(see Chapter 14)

Wake up early or sleep in. Take a walk along the beach or just enjoy the view from your room. But make sure you check out of your hotel in time to leave for the stadium around 10:30 or 11:00 a.m.

While the ballpark is brand new, the history of the Philadelphia Phillies in Clearwater goes way back. They've been training in this community since 1948. Enjoy exploring the new park. Get some autographs, watch practice and the game, eat a cheese steak sandwich, and listen to the stories of those who have been coming to Clearwater for decades.

After the game, hop in your car and head back down to SR 60. Take it to I-275 east. Then take I-4 east (toward Orlando) to Lakeland. Pull off at Exit 32 (U.S. 98) in Lakeland and check into a roadside hotel (see Chapter 7). It won't be fancy, but it will make for a fast getaway in the morning. You'll find a lot of restaurants and a mall near U.S. 98. If you would like to do some sightseeing, head over to Florida Southern College and give yourself a self-guided tour of its 12 Frank Lloyd Wright buildings (see Chapter 7 "Attractions").

Day Seven: Joker Marchant Stadium / Tigers
(see Chapter 7)

You'll be heading home tonight, but you've got one more baseball stop first. The Detroit Tigers and Lakeland have the longest association of any team and community in the Grapefruit League — 73 years. The Tigers have spent 40 of them at this stadium. You wouldn't guess the stadium was that old, though. It looks very modern thanks to renovations made in 2002.

Since this is your last chance to enjoy the Florida sun, pull out a blanket and sit on the berm. If you arrive early, you can snag balls from batting practice. Then enjoy the game for a few hours while you soak up the heat.

It's about a two-hour drive to the Orlando International Airport, but you might want to leave some extra time in case there is traffic. Take I-4 to the Central Florida Greeneway, (Exit 62 East). It's a toll road that will take you directly to the south entrance of the airport.

Option: If you can squeeze in another vacation day, spend Day Six enjoying the Clearwater area and visit Bright House Networks Field and Joker Marchant Stadium on Days Seven and Eight. Here are some suggestions for ways to spend your optional day that tie in with this itinerary's "History" theme:

Optional Day Six: At Leisure
(see Chapters 14 through 17)

This is a day to explore some non-baseball facets of the Sunshine State — fishing, golf, historic sites, museums, shopping, or just more time on the beach.

Try your hand at one of Florida's oldest pastimes, fishing. The Gulf of Mexico has some wonderful fishing spots, and boats and guides are available at a range of rates. This is the easiest type of fishing around. You put a piece of squid on your hook and drop the line until it hits the bottom. While you usually won't get big fish, you will get a lot of fish.

You can go out on "party boat," which is open to all comers, for a half-day or full-day trip. The cost is usually $50 or less and includes all tackle and bait, plus help from the crew. Some boats throw in lunch. The fishing is better on the full-day trips. If you prefer to be more exclusive, you can charter a boat for yourself and your family. This typically runs about $600 a day. You'll catch bigger fish and you won't be elbow to elbow with strangers. Again, the ship's crew will assist you in all your fishing needs or leave you alone, as you wish.

If fishing isn't your thing, you can play golf at one of several great courses or trek down to Fort Desoto Park, where you will find one of Florida's oldest forts and great beaches (see Chapter 16). Or make this a museum day. You'll find three in downtown St. Pete: the Salvador Dali Museum (see Chapter 16), the Florida International Museum (244 Second Avenue North, 727-341-7900, www.floridamuseum.org), and The Florida Holocaust Museum (55 Fifth Street, 727-820-0100, www.flholocaustmuseum.org)

You're also close to Busch Gardens Africa. That doesn't fit in with the theme of this trip, but if it appeals to you, see Day Four of Itinerary One and Chapter 13 for more information.

Itinerary Three:
Baseball and Boardwalks

This trip combines theme park thrills with America's favorite pastime. You'll spend most of your time in the Orlando and Tampa metro areas and have plenty of time for sightseeing. Compared with the other itineraries, you might call this one baseball lite, because you will visit only three ballparks.

Flexibility: This itinerary is fairly flexible because it is centered on just two areas. However, all three ballparks are popular, so you will want to get your tickets before you head to Florida, preferably in January or early February.

Tip: Be sure to reserve your rental car and first three nights' hotel room when you make your plane reservations, especially if you are coming in mid to late March. Orlando's tourist traffic swells with vacationing families and college students then thanks to school and college Spring Breaks, and I am suggesting you spend your first three nights at Disney's All-Star Sports Resort, a popular value-priced property.

Book a late afternoon or evening return flight to leave time for a half-day visit to one more attraction before leaving for the airport.

Day One: Walt Disney World Resort (WDW)

Arrive at Orlando International Airport, rent your car, and drive to WDW. The most direct route is via the Central Florida Greeneway (south airport exit). It is a toll road, but it will take you directly to Osceola Parkway, which intersects with a well-marked road that will take you directly to WDW's All-Star Resorts. Check in at Disney's All-Star Sports Resort. The rooms are small, but it is the best value on Disney property and we're sticking with a theme here. There are several nicer hotels on property if you want to spend more money and plenty of cheaper hotels off property.

You can spend the remainder of the day at one of WDW's water parks, playing putt-putt, or walking around Downtown Disney (see Chapter 2 "Attractions").

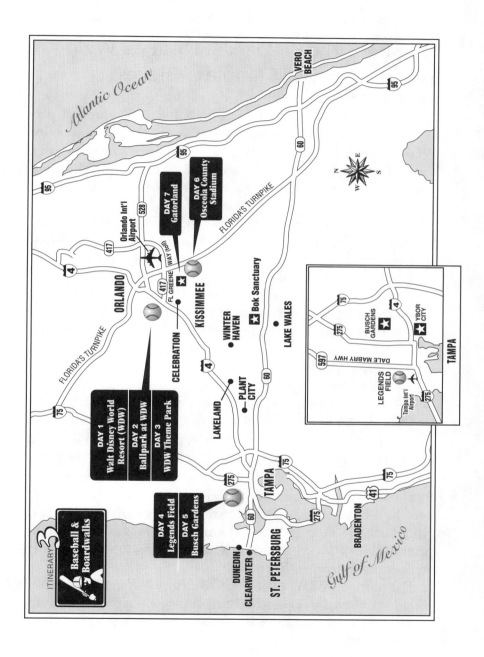

There are lots of restaurants on Disney property all of which are very good. My personal favorite is Portobello Yacht Club, located at Downtown Disney near Pleasure Island.

Day Two: The Ballpark at Disney's Wide World of Sports® Complex / Braves
(see Chapter 2)

It's time to head out to your first baseball game of this trip. It's not far. Enjoy breakfast at the hotel and then board WDW's free bus to the complex. Leave an hour or so to work through the bus system. Or drive your rental car. The complex is just a short distance away, off Osceola Parkway, and parking is free.

This stadium is not a traditional Spring Training park, but you'll enjoy baseball Disney style. There are lots of food options here and you might want to try lunch at the All-Star Café next door to the stadium.

When you're done with baseball, head to Pleasure Island for your nighttime experience. Or have a wonderful dinner at the California Grill at the top of Disney's Contemporary Resort. It's one of the best places to watch the Magic Kingdom's nightly fireworks.

Day Three: WDW Theme Park

It's time to visit a WDW theme park. There are four to choose from, each appealing to a certain type of visitor. If you've never been to Walt Disney World, you should certainly visit the Magic Kingdom. It was the first Disney theme park in Florida and the one that made this place famous. If you've been to WDW before, you may want to explore Disney's Animal Kingdom, the newest WDW theme park. Movie buffs might prefer Disney-MGM Studios, while many adults, especially seniors, head toward Epcot.

For more on WDW, check out *The Hassle-Free Walt Disney World Vacation*, by Steven M. Barrett (www.TheOtherOrlando. com). It includes customized touring plans for each of the four parks as well as information and insider tips on the hotels, restaurants, and attractions.

Day Four: Legends Field / Yankees
(see Chapter 13)

You're going to pack up early and head to Tampa for a game at Legends Field. Seeing the New York Yankees at their Spring Training home is the closest thing to a theme-park experience that baseball has to offer. It's about a two-hour drive if traffic holds up. So allow yourself two and a half hours just to be on the safe side.

Take I-4 from WDW to Tampa. Follow signs to St. Petersburg when you get to the intersection of I-4 and I-275. When you get to Dale Mabry (exit 41B), turn right (north). Legends Field is about three miles along, on your left.

Legends Field is the largest stadium in the Grapefruit League and the most like a Major League Baseball stadium. Enjoy the game and make sure you try the Bloomin' Onions from the Outback Steakhouse concession at the stadium.

Afterwards head toward Busch Gardens. Drive north on Dale Mabry about four miles and take a right onto Busch Boulevard. Busch Gardens is about five miles along, on your left. Check in to a hotel near the park. There are several in the area.

If you want to go out tonight, go to Ybor City near downtown Tampa for good food and nightlife. (It's just south of I-4 and east of I-275.) Dubbed "Florida's Latin Quarter," it's a National Historic Landmark District packed with bars, restaurants, shops, and entertainment. The nation's first cigar factories were located here and you can still buy hand-rolled cigars in Ybor City shops.

If you prefer gambling, head for Derby Lane, the greyhound track in St. Pete (I-275 south to exit 28, Gandy Boulevard). Post time is 7:30 p.m. (see Chapter 16 "Attractions").

Day Five: Busch Gardens Africa
(see Chapter 13, "Attractions")

Get set. This park has five roller coasters, more than any other park in Florida. It also has wonderful animal exhibits, other rides, and theater shows. You'll probably want to spend the entire day here. When you get done, get back in your car and drive back toward Orlando. Stop in Kissimmee and check into a hotel for two nights. A great choice is the Gaylord Palms (see Chapter 9) at the intersection of Osceola Parkway and I-4, to the east of the Interstate. You can't miss it. It is the only hotel you will see at this intersection.

Day Six: Osceola County Stadium / Astros
(see Chapter 9)

Wake up and enjoy breakfast at any one of the wonderful restaurants at the Gaylord Palms. Its huge atrium is divided into different regions of Florida. My personal favorite is the ship in the Key West area. Other areas include a swamp and a Spanish fort like the one in St. Augustine. You have a couple of options on what you can do this morning before heading over to the stadium and your final Spring Training game. Perhaps you would like to take a helicopter tour over Walt Disney World Resort and Universal Orlando. You'll find a number of small heli-tour operators right within a few miles of the hotel on West Irlo Bronson Memorial Highway (U.S. 192), en route to the stadium. Or spend an hour walking through Old Town, a shopping center about a mile from the Gaylord Palms on West Irlo Bronson. You'll find funky stores, a roller coaster, several amusement park rides, and some restaurants and coffee shops.

Whatever your choice of activity, make sure you leave for the stadium at about 11:30 a.m. It is about a 25-minute drive from the Gaylord Palms on U.S. 192; so you'll make it in plenty of time for the game. There's no need to come earlier because most autographs will be found after the game.

Osceola County Stadium is going to be the exact opposite of what you've experienced so far. You've been to the largest and second largest stadiums in the Grapefruit League. Now, you're going to the smallest. It's up to you to determine which is the better experience.

After you've gotten as many autographs as you want, drive to Celebration, a town designed and built by The Walt Disney Company. Here you'll find shops and some very good restaurants — try the paella at the Columbia Restaurant. It's great to walk around Celebration's downtown area and then enjoy the rocking chairs on the porch of the Celebration Hotel.

Day Seven: Gatorland

After breakfast, check out of your hotel and head east on Osceola Parkway to U.S. 441 Turn north (left). Gatorland will be on your right about 1.4 miles up the road.

This is a great half-day attraction. Gatorland offers a wonderful alligator habitat, along with alligator wrestling (man vs. beast), and the "Gator Jumparoo." No trip to Florida is complete without watching enormous gators leaping awkwardly out of the water to try to snag raw chickens.

When you wrap up at Gatorland, head north to the Central Florida Greeneway (SR 417) and turn east (right). The Greeneway will take you directly to the Orlando International Airport's south entrance.

Itinerary Four:
The Gulf Coast

This trip along Florida's Gulf Coast is perhaps the most scenic of the five itineraries. You will experience great baseball and great beaches, breathtaking views and coconut palms. You'll visit five ballparks and get to see two of the marquee teams in their Spring Training homes. When you're not at the ballpark, you'll have your choice of activities and attractions ranging from golf and fishing to shopping, museums, and sunbathing on some of Florida's nicest beaches.

Flexibility: Plan ahead to make sure the game schedules work before you finalize your travel dates. You can easily switch around days two, three, and four, which are all in the Fort Myers area. You can also switch days five and six, which are near Sarasota. But it will be hard to switch in any other way. Also, get your Red Sox and Yankees tickets as soon as you can, preferably in early January.

Note: This itinerary calls for flying into Fort Myers and out of Tampa. If you prefer to fly in and out of the same airport, book a night flight for your return to allow time for the 130-mile or so drive back to the airport on Day Seven. Either way, rent a car with unlimited mileage.

Day One: Tamiami Trail, Fort Myers

Fly into Southwest Florida International Airport, rent your car, and drive to the Best Western Waterfront (see Chapter 4), where you will spend three nights. It's located in downtown Fort Myers and is a great stepping off point for baseball in the area. You'll probably be tired from the flight, so enjoy dinner at one of the many restaurants down the Tamiami Trail. It's the main street in Fort Myers. If you arrive early and have the energy, take in some of the local sights.

Note: If you don't already have tickets for tomorrow's Red Sox game at City of Palms Park, drive over and try to get them today. Be forewarned. You may well find that standing room is all that's available because the park nearly always sells out.

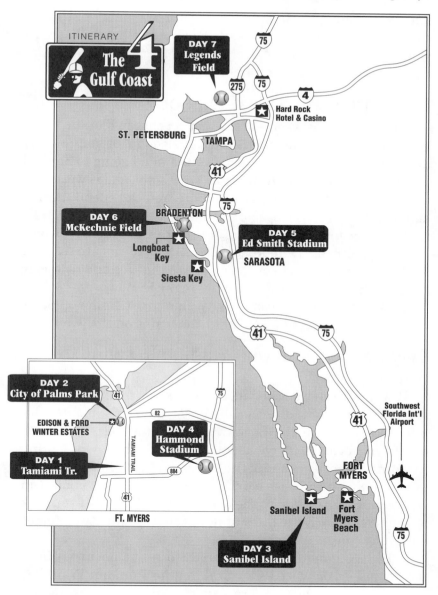

Day Two: City of Palms Park / Red Sox
(see Chapter 4)

Get up early to give yourself time to see the winter homes of Thomas Edison and Henry Ford before you head for the ballpark. The Edison-Ford Winter Estates open at 9:00 a.m. Get there at opening and take the first tour. Make sure you leave by around 11:30 a.m. to give yourself plenty of time at the ballpark. After the game, go back to the hotel. Wash up, change clothes, and head over to Fort Myers Beach, about 30 minutes away, for a nice dinner on the water.

Day Three: The Great Outdoors

Fort Myers boasts some of the best beaches in Florida. Today is the day to check them out. You can sleep in, or get up early and enjoy sunrise on the beach. I recommend going to Sanibel Island. It is about 45 minutes from your hotel, and is worth the drive because there is a lot to do there. You can spend the day simply relaxing on the beach. Or soak up the sun and then take in the shops and eat in the boutique restaurants. There is nice kayaking here for the more athletic as well as nature trails to explore. If you like to fish, you can go to the pier and test your luck. You must bring your own fishing pole, however.

Whatever your choice of activity, plan to eat dinner on Sanibel, so you that don't have to fight the traffic on the way back.

Day Four: Hammond Stadium / Twins
(see Chapter 11)

It's time for more baseball. You can sleep in and still make it to Hammond Stadium in plenty of time. It's about a 45-minute drive from the Best Western Waterfront, so plan to check out in time to leave about 10:30 a.m. The Twins Spring Training home is not one of the better stadiums in the League, but it is one of the best looking on the outside. It is built in the architectural style of the area, with a tin roof. If you look around as you drive to the stadium, you'll see plenty of homes with matching roof styles.

After the game, drive up to Sarasota. It's about an hour north via I-75 or twice as long taking the Tamiami Trail. The Trail is not that much more scenic than the Interstate, but you'll get a look at several Florida small towns.

Check in for two nights at one of the Sarasota hotels listed in Chapter 5. When you're ready for dinner, drive over to Siesta Key. You'll find a fantastic shopping area in the round that has plenty of upscale restaurants and a wonderful candy factory with the longest line for ice cream you'll see anywhere.

Day Five: Ed Smith Stadium / Reds
(see Chapter 5)

Wake up early to enjoy one of Sarasota's great attractions. Go to the traffic circle in Siesta Key and head north toward Longboat Key. Very quickly, you'll see the Mote Marine Laboratory, home to Mote Aquarium. This is a fantastic aquarium with a large shark exhibit and two manatees, Hugh and Buffet. These large water mammals are endangered species and beloved by many. You'll find it easy to fall in love with these gentle giants.

Make sure you leave by noon to get to the ballpark by gametime — and bring an appetite. You don't need to arrive early because it is very difficult to get autographs at Ed Smith Stadium. But you should save room for the Big Red Smokey. This smoked sausage is the culinary highlight when you are watching the Cincinnati Reds play in Sarasota.

What you do after the game depends on whether you are lucky enough to be in Sarasota during the annual county fair in mid March. If so, by all means go. If not, I would suggest going back to St. Armands Key and enjoying a wonderful dinner at the Columbia Restaurant.

Day Six: McKechnie Field / Pirates
(see Chapter 15)

This is your day to go to Bradenton's McKechnie Field, one of the top parks in the Grapefruit League. After breakfast, check out of your hotel and drive to Bradenton. It's about 20 miles north of central Sarasota on U.S. 41. McKechnie Field can be difficult to find, so leave some extra time to make sure you get to the park a couple of hours before gametime. You will want plenty of time to soak up the scenery and get autographs. You'll get a lot of signatures here.

After the game, drive to I-75 and head north to Tampa. You'll find the Seminole Hard Rock Hotel & Casino at the junction of I-75 and I-4 (see Chapter 13 "Attractions"). Bed down there for the last night of your Spring Training vacation if they have rooms available. A stay in a Hard Rock property is always fun. If you can't get in there, check the "Hotels" section of Chapter 13 for other possibilities.

Day Seven: Legends Field / Yankees
(see Chapter 13)

This is the day you head home, but before you go, try to take in a game at Legends Field. It's not the prettiest stadium in the league or the quaintest, but it is an experience. After all, it is the largest Grapefruit League stadium and as the Yankees never tire of reminding you, the Spring Training home of the team that's won the World Series more times than any other. The stadium is practically next door to Tampa International Airport. So you can leave early if needed to catch your flight home.

Itinerary Five:
The East Coast

A baseball trip down Florida's east coast provides the traveler with the best mix of all that Florida has to offer. This trip takes you to four ballparks, two of them historic, one a newer, yet fan-friendly stadium, and one that tries too much to be a Major League clone. You'll get to watch the stars warm up and stand next to some of today's top players. Along the way, you'll experience two charming small coastal towns, Vero Beach and Port St. Lucie, where life is a little slower and the people relaxed, and two of Florida's largest cities, Fort Lauderdale and West Palm Beach, with their multimillion dollar beach houses and hectic pace. The two types of cities contrast nearly as much as the baseball stadiums in their shadows.

This is the tour of the stars, where you never know whom you'll run into and what diamond experiences will become lifelong memories.

Flexibility: While you can easily switch days four and five, it will be hard to switch any other days without spending most of your non-ballpark time on the road. So again, check the game schedules when they come out in mid December and plan your trip accordingly.

You'll fly in and out of Palm Beach International Airport on this itinerary, because it is midway between Vero Beach and Fort Lauderdale, your most northerly and southerly destinations.

Tip: Get tickets early for Fort Lauderdale Stadium (Baltimore Orioles). You don't want to miss the box seats there; they are the most comfortable seats in the Grapefruit League. You will also want to get tickets early for Roger Dean Stadium in Jupiter, especially if the St. Louis Cardinals are scheduled to play on the day of your visit. And, if you want to spend your first night at Disney's Vero Beach Resort, as I recommend, book it early.

Note: You may want to bring along your passport or a certified copy of your birth certificate in case you decide to visit the Bahamas on Day Four.

Day One: Vero Beach

Fly into Palm Beach International Airport in West Palm Beach. It's about as close to the center of this itinerary as you're going to get. Rent a car and get on I-95 North to Vero Beach. It's about 65 miles away and will take you about an hour and a half.

When you get there, you'll want to stay on the beach. While there are several nice hotels, a fantastic place to stay is Disney's Vero Beach Resort (9250 Island Grove Terrace, U.S. A1A, Vero Beach; 772-234-2000). It's a little north of Vero Beach on U.S. A1A, but it's worth the extra drive.

Enjoy a nice dinner in Vero Beach and then take a long walk on the beach. It's one of the few places in Florida that is still a nearly natural beach.

Day Two: Dodgertown / Dodgers
(see Chapter 10)

Get up very early today, around 6:00 a.m., and walk out to the beach for a beautiful Florida sunrise. You haven't seen anything until you've watched the sun creep up from the water. It looks like it is coming up from a swim.

Enjoy the beach, eat breakfast, and then check out of your hotel and make your way to Dodgertown. You'll want to get there early to experience everything this historic park has to offer. Plan to arrive around 9:30 a.m. or so and spend your morning walking around the practice fields. You'll observe the difference between the minor league players and the Major League players. You'll listen to the stars as they play games and warm up together. And you'll leave the fields with a new appreciation for the stars of today's game.

The game itself starts at 1:00 p.m., but you'll want to position yourself near the stadium between 11:00 a.m. and noon. That's when the players walk to the stadium from the practice fields. If you're standing nearby, you'll have great opportunities for autographs and chances to talk to some of baseball's great players. When you do go inside, go right to the concession stand and buy a Dodger Dog. It's one of baseball's great treats.

After the game, you're going to head back to I-95 and south

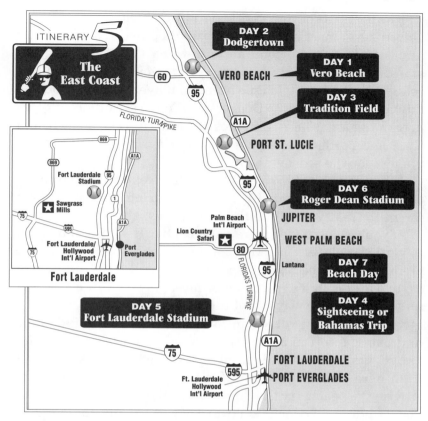

to Port St. Lucie. There is not much to do at night in Port St. Lucie, so consider your options. If you want to get a hotel on the beach you can. The beach is actually Hutchinson Island, and you'll find a very nice Marriott there (the Hutchinson Island Marriott Beach Resort & Marina, 555 Northeast Ocean Boulevard, Stuart; 772-225-3700). However, it's about 20 miles from the ballpark and you'll want to be at the stadium early tomorrow. So I would recommend staying near the Interstate.

Day Three: Tradition Field / Mets
(see Chapter 12)

Wake up around 7:30 a.m., check out of your hotel, and grab some breakfast. You'll want to be at the ballpark by around 9:00 a.m. You're seeing the New York Mets today, so get your attitude pumping and start acting like you "heart" New York.

The best part of your visit to Tradition Field happens hours before the game. The team opens up its practice fields to fans and invites them to come in and watch the routines of the stars. Just as you did yesterday, you're going to see what it's really like to be a big league baseball player. But you won't be duplicating your visit to Dodgertown. You'll see different types of training areas here from those you saw at Dodgertown, and thus, get a different perspective on how teams prepare their players for the season ahead.

When the box office opens, pay a little extra for a box seat; they are the best seats in the park. During the game, don't forget to treat yourself to the Italian ices.

If you're looking for more autographs after the game, walk toward the players' parking lot on the northwest side of the stadium. You'll be able to spot it, as it will have a bunch of luxury automobiles in it. Sometimes, players will come over and sign on their way out of the park.

After the game, drive an hour south to Fort Lauderdale and check into the Marriott on North Andrews Avenue for two nights. It is centrally located and you'll find it easy to get from here to most places in South Florida. If you prefer to stay on the beach, try the Sheraton Yankee Trader (321 North Fort Lauderdale Beach Boulevard, U.S. A1A, Fort Lauderdale; 954-467-1111).

Either way, you'll want to spend the evening on the beach. You might eat at a restaurant in BeachPlace, a shopping, dining, and entertainment complex two blocks north of Las Olas Boulevard on Fort Lauderdale Beach Boulevard (A1A) and about two miles north of Port Everglades. But the restaurants elsewhere on A1A offer a much better view of the action on Fort Lauderdale Beach. Many of them have tables on the sidewalk, and it's exciting to watch the different types of people who cruise the Fort Lauderdale strip.

Day Four: Rest, Sightseeing, or Bahamas Cruise

Today is a day for rest, sports, or sightseeing. You can go to the beach or visit Lion Country Safari, a drive-through preserve with over 900 animals. You can shop at Sawgrass Mills, one of the largest malls in the world. You can walk the tree-lined streets of Los Olas Boulevard, the Melrose Drive of the southeast. You can indulge your passion for golf or fishing. There are wonderful golf courses here, and you're only a short boat ride from the Gulf Stream and some of the best fishing in the world.

However, I would suggest you spend the day in the Bahamas. One of the neat things about Fort Lauderdale is that it is only 50 miles from the island chain, so you can get there on a short, inexpensive, one-day cruise.

If you want to experience the islands, Discovery Cruise Line offers a daily cruise. It leaves Port Everglades at 7:45 a.m. and arrives in Freeport, Bahamas at 1:00 p.m. You get a huge breakfast and lunch on the way to Freeport, along with casino games, lounge chairs, and a swimming pool. In Freeport, you can go to the beautiful beaches, walk around the Caribbean market, or play in yet another casino. Make sure you're back on the ship by 4:45 p.m. for the return trip. You'll have a wonderful dinner and evening under the stars and arrive back in Fort Lauderdale at around 10:00 p.m.

Note: To take the trip you must have either a passport or a certified copy of your birth certificate plus a driver's license. The cruise costs under $150 per person.

Day Five: Fort Lauderdale Stadium / Orioles
(see Chapter 3)

Today you're going to see the Baltimore Orioles. Sleep in from your busy day. Then get up, check out of the hotel, and drop by the Starlite Diner for breakfast on your way to the ballpark. Plan on getting to the park around 11:00 a.m. so you can watch batting practice and get autographs.

The key to enjoying Fort Lauderdale Stadium and the Baltimore Orioles is to buy your tickets early and get a box seat. The single best feature of the stadium is the legroom in the box seats. You have about a yard between you and the seat in front of you — plenty of room to stretch even the longest legs. The seats are sunny, but they are the most comfortable I've found in all of sports.

After the game, take I-95 north to West Palm Beach. On the way, stop to eat at Riggins Crabhouse. It's just off the Interstate in Lantana, about 12 miles south of West Palm Beach. It specializes in blue crabs, which are harder and harder to come by these days as populations of the sea creature dwindle. You'll find some of the best here. Order them steamed and prepare to get messy.

When you get to West Palm Beach (about 30 minutes from Riggins), stay at the West Palm Beach Marriott (1001 Okeechobee Boulevard; 561-833-1234). It's near the Interstate, at the edge of downtown West Palm Beach, making for a quick getaway in the mornings. Check in for two nights.

Day Six: Roger Dean Stadium / Cardinals & Marlins
(see Chapter 8)

The ballpark is about 20 minutes north, on I-95 in Jupiter. You can eat breakfast at the hotel or travel west to the International House of Pancakes and other restaurants, but don't linger too long over coffee. You'll want to get to the ballpark early, as this is a wonderful, fan-friendly park.

Note: Make sure you bring — and wear — sunscreen. You will be sitting in the sun for at least part of the game wherever your seats are located.

Tip: Keep an eye on your surroundings, because you never know who you will run into here. Several movie stars live in the Jupiter area and enjoy getting out to a ballgame. When I was in Jupiter, I met actor John Goodman.

After the game, return to the hotel and wash up. You'll be spending a night on the town. About a mile to the east is City Place, an upscale shopping, dining, and entertainment center. It has some fantastic restaurants and a giant movie theater.

Day Seven: Beach

You're going home today, but hopefully you left enough time to spend a little more time on the beach. It's easy to get to and it will be fun to soak up some rays before you leave sunny Florida.

Chapter 21

Index 1.

Index To Stadiums and Itineraries

Photo by Kelly Monaghan.

Play ball! What better way to enjoy a bright spring day than in a Grapefruit League ballpark like Clearwater's Bright House Networks Field. The sun is warm, the players are close, the food and drink are tasty, and fans can often get autographs.

Index 2.

Index To Teams and Itineraries

Free Updates

For free updates to this book and other Intrepid Traveler books about the many attractions of Central Florida, visit:

http://www.TheOtherOrlando.com/updates/

Other Books from The Intrepid Traveler

The Intrepid Traveler publishes money-saving, horizon expanding travel how-to and guidebooks dedicated to helping its readers make world travel an integral part of their everyday life.

In addition, we offer hard-to-find specialty books from other publishers. For more information visit our web site, where you will find a complete catalog, frequent updates to this and other of our books, travel articles from around the world, Internet travel resources, and more:

http://www.IntrepidTraveler.com

If you are interested in becoming a home-based travel agent, visit the Home-Based Travel Agent Resource Center at:

http://www.HomeTravelAgency.com